# A Strange Vocation
## Independent Bishops Tell Their Stories

EDITED BY ALISTAIR BATE

Contributors:
Markus van Alphen | Ken Babauta
Alistair Bate | Jonathan Blake
Timothy Cravens | Richard Gundrey
Aristid Havlicek | John Kersey
Ronald Langham | John Mabry
Rosamonde Miller | John Plummer
River Sims | Elizabeth Stuart | Alexis Tancibok
Carol Vaccariello | Wynn Wagner

the apocryphile press
BERKELEY, CA
www.apocryphile.org

*This book is respectfully dedicated to the memory of
The Rt. Rev. Johannes van Alphen 1925–2009,
a loving father in God and an elder statesman
of the Liberal Catholic movement.*

Apocryphile Press
1700 Shattuck Ave #81
Berkeley, CA 94709
www.apocryphile.org

Printed in the United States of America
ISBN 1-933993-75-8

# Contents

# Introduction

WELCOME READER, WHETHER YOU be "one of our own"—a member of the Independent Sacramental Movement (ISM)—or whether you be a member of another Christian family, or indeed a curious non-Christian. This little book is a gift from the heart of the "Indie" movement to you and we hope that in some way, you will find it edifying. If you wish to become better informed about our movement, you should find this collection enlightening and if you currently seek a spiritual family, you may well find here what you seek.

This book is one of a series of books published in recent years by members of the Independent Sacramental Movement ourselves, with a twofold purpose. Firstly, we hope to edify and encourage each other in these uniquely creative ways of being church and secondly, we hope to make our movement better known and understood amongst the general public and particularly our brothers and sisters in Christ in the mainstream denominations.

We recognise that for some readers this book might be

a first introduction to our movement, and that there are inevitable questions that will therefore come to mind. The reader may ask: What distinguishes the independent movement? What is its theological stance? Who are its clergy, and where do they worship? This book provides a series of individual answers to these questions. There are yet more answers that would come forth from the diversity of the ISM, and precious little in the way of useful or precise generalisation. Yet some common patterns are certainly observable.

Within my own tradition of Catholic liberalism, we are inevitably perceived by the public as standing in the shadow of Rome. The first preconception to overcome is that we are, in fact, independent of Papal jurisdiction although still very much a part of the One Holy Catholic and Apostolic Church. Not only this, but we are far from a new movement, instead tracing our differences with the Holy See to the First Vatican Council of 1870, and in some cases to even earlier developments. With freedom from the dogma imposed by Rome comes the freedom to rediscover the gifts of the early Church as well as to be directed by the Spirit in our own times; to understand Catholicism as an inherently liberal movement and our God as a God of love and not of judgement.

The origins of Independent Catholicism are varied and diverse, deriving either from the Papal line or from the Orthodox churches. The most visible of the historic Independent Catholic figures at the turn of the twentieth-century, Arnold Harris Mathew and Joseph René Vilatte, received the Catholic episcopate in the successions of the Old Catholics of Utrecht and the Jacobite Patriarchate of Antioch respectively. More generally, the Ultrajectine developments that characterise the emergent ISM at this period should be seen in the context of the triumph of the Ultramontanists at the First Vatican Council and the resulting tensions concerning Papal infallibility.

Yet this is not the full story. ISM bishops in some cases trace their ancestry to much more recent differences with Rome, such as those whose orders come from the Brazilian Catholic Apostolic Church, formed by Roman Catholic bishop Carlos Duarte Costa in protest against the Vatican's alliance with the Nazi regime during World War II. Others are of Protestant origin, or derive from unification movements such as the Catholicate of the West led by Mar Georgius. Some are strongly traditionalist, and see their primary theological purpose as to continue the true Church of Rome in the face of the perceived heresy of Vatican II or sometimes much earlier theological developments. Others are esotericists, seeking a Christianity open to the insights of other faiths and philosophies, and drawing upon the widest possible range of influences both from existing theology and from society at large. The greater number of bishops who have contributed to this book fall into this latter category.

Theological positions, even within the more liberal sector of the ISM, tend to diverge based on episcopal polity; the bishop who leads an independent community has arguably a greater direct influence on its interpretation of the deposit of faith than any pope in history. There tends to be variance between communities on the issues of the ordination of women, married clergy and the ordination of sexually active gay and lesbian people, and these administrative matters are then further complicated by a range of theological positions that stretches from those who actively seek reunion with a Holy Mother Church freed from what are seen as its present errors, to those who hold that unity is a lesser priority than the expression of individual or collective conscience in creating a community in which the voice of God may be heard. There is truly something for everyone.

While many clergy and lay folk familiar with the established denominations identify "church" with those buildings purpose-built for worship, the ISM remains harder to find. Certainly there are churches in existence, ranging from at least one magnificent cathedral to more modest churches and chapels, and increasingly, rented communal spaces within buildings not primarily intended as religious centres. Yet people will need to make an effort to seek them out and to join communities that, while often tight-knit to the outside world's perception, are in fact friendly and welcoming once they have established that the visitor is there for the same purposes as themselves. There is a good deal of worship through home oratories, converted outbuildings and unadvertised Mass centres where the faithful congregate, knowing that "where two or three are gathered, there am I in the midst of them." And this flexibility of location also creates a flexibility of outlook; a means to explore the changing nature of what "being church" means, and how that concept can evolve to meet the needs of Christ in our world today.

Bishops John Plummer and John Mabry in their excellent introductory booklet "Who are the Independent Catholics?" describe four main groupings or "families", within the Independent Sacramental Movement which they helpfully label; Traditionalist, Liberal, Esoteric and Syncretistic. It might be as well for the reader to keep these categories in mind and notice into which group or groups each of the contributors to this book might fit—and most of us will defy easy classification!

On the matter of syncretism, many of the contributors have disclosed their "own particular mix" for the reader, for example, our publisher Bishop John Mabry helpfully summarised, "...if pinned to the wall, I will admit that my cosmology is Whiteheadian, my theology, Unitarian; my Christology, Arian; my soteriology, Abelardian and universalist. But my worship tradition is Catholic, specifically, Anglo-Catholic." Though the content of each of our individually-evolved theologies might be very various the obvious syncretism of Bishop Mabry's summary is fairly typical of ISM clergy, and could well be fairly typical of most non-fundamentalist clergy, even in mainline denominations, if they were in a position to freely admit it.

However, some of our contributing Bishops are less syncretistic than others, for example Bishop Tim Cravens prioritises "Sound Doctrine" in his list of six necessary elements for a healthy Independent Catholic life and he also acknowledges that his "vision as a Bishop has always been to adhere to Christian orthodoxy." For moderate traditionalists such as Bishop Tim the liberal tendency is seen more in the area of ethics than theology. However, for many of us who might feel part of the "esoteric" family, the traditionalist impulse manifests in our high regard for the traditional rites of Christendom which we would regard as greater vehicles of sacramental power than rites such as, for example, the Novus Ordo of Roman Catholicism. Perhaps uniquely, in our movement this liturgical traditionalism is often combined with the greatest theological freedom. This is particularly the case within "Liberal

Catholic" jurisdictions, represented in this book by Bishops Stuart, Mugleston, Havlicek and Van Alphen, as well as the Church of Antioch (represented by Archbishop Gundrey), the Liberal Catholic Apostolic Church (represented by Mar Joannes III and myself) and the Ecclesia Gnostica Mysteriorum of Bishop Rosamonde Miller.

Lest the reader think that ISM Bishops are totally preoccupied with worship and theology, let me also reassure you that among the Bishops here represented you will read about exciting and innovative ministries which make a huge practical difference in people's lives. Such, for example is Bishop River Sim's "Catholic Worker" inspired ministry in San Francisco. But whether, for example, through +River's street-level needle exchange, or the hospitality charism followed by Bishop Liz Stuart in imitation of St. Brigid of Kildare, or the Franciscan charism as lived by Archbishop Ron Langham, all of us in our several ways try to meet Christ in others, and be Christ to others, as best we can. Such, after all, is the essence of the Gospel. St. James said "Religion that is pure and undefiled before God, the father, is this: to care for orphans and widows in their distress, and to keep oneself unstained by the world" (James 1:27).

This is a book of vocational stories. Even in our great diversity, one of the things we ISM Bishops have in common is the belief that we have been called by God to our various ministries. I hope and pray that within these pages the discerning reader may be able to trace God's hand at work. What we may ask does God hope to achieve by calling such a colourful group of people to the grace of the fullness of Holy Orders? Well, we may be certain that it is not solely for the benefit of ourselves and the people we currently reach through our various ministries. Could it be that the Church as the Mystical Body of Christ in the future will be a body which values and affirms diversity and values and affirms each individual member regardless of his or her gender, sexuality or even creed? If so, then the Independent Sacramental Movement will have a huge part to play!

Thank you, reader, for buying this book. A large proportion of the royalties will be sent to the children's charity, Plan International. We hope you enjoy our stories and we pray that you will find some enlightenment and inspiration and may also feel called to make further exploration of the Independent Sacramental Movement.

Blessings on your journey,

*+Alistair Bate CCP,*
*Mar Alexei,*
*Titular Bishop of Hebron,*
*Liberal Catholic Apostolic Church*

"Where the Spirit of the Lord is, there is liberty."
—2nd Corinthians 3: 17

The Rt. Rev.
Markus van Alphen

The Young Rite

# "Towards a New Priesthood"

I WAS BORN IN 1960 IN PRETORIA, South Africa, into a theosophical family. Since my father was a priest in the Liberal Catholic Church, I was born into the church, in a manner of speaking. As a young toddler, I would laze around on the floor whilst my father or some visiting priest or bishop celebrated the Eucharist. I can vaguely remember the sun beams shining through the windows, creating coloured shafts of light in the incense still hanging in the air. The "zing" of a well-celebrated Eucharist, that very particular atmosphere that was built up, was quite normal for me. Being the third of four boys, it was natural that as I grew up I would follow my elder brothers in becoming an altar boy, which I did. Religion and the church to me were not a matter of choice, but a matter of practice. Little boys become big boys and as a healthy teenager does, I went in search of my own identity, leaving church, theosophy, and everything to do with spirituality behind me. A family and my career as an electrical engineer became priorities. Several years later my interest in religious matters gradually returned. In the mean time I had settled in the Netherlands, where I returned to the Liberal Catholic Church, was ordained to the priesthood, joined the Theosophical Society, its Esoteric School, the Order of the Round Table, Freemasonry, Martinism, and other ritual or theosophically-minded bodies. I became a sponge and wanted to know everything. Avidly, I read anything I could get my hands on. Both the Dutch and the International magazines of the Liberal Catholic Church were in need of an editor, a gap I filled with enthusiasm.

As an adult, the choice I had made this time was a conscious one. The theosophical tenets were—as they still are—as natural to me as breathing. Recognizing the many religions as different ways to the same state of enlightenment, adding the theosophical teachings to Christianity gave me the key to understanding the power of ritual. God was no longer the bearded man on a cloud of which my religious instruction teacher had tried to convince me. On the contrary, in God we live and move and have our being—the transcendent Trinity. In every human being the Christ Light shines—God immanent. From this sprouts a far greater duality to me than the duality in the flesh between masculine and feminine.

God is transcendent as well as immanent and especially this second aspect intrigued me. Religion became to me what its Latin root means—binding back—or connecting to that inner source. The reconnection is the dissolving of the Great Duality, the AtOneMent, or initiation. Ritual is symbol and symbol represents a dynamic truth that cannot effectively be captured in words. Being a part of, or better still taking an active role in a ritual gives me the feeling of connection with that symbol and its underlying truth. In short, the symbolism of the Christian tradition and its representation in the church year, the Eucharist and the sacraments evoke an experience within me. Searching within that experience is for me the true initiation.

Ritual is a form of magic. I can still remember the shiver going up and down my spine during the three verses of the Litany sung by the bishop during the ordinations to sub-deacon, deacon, and priest. The same shiver goes up and down my spine today when, as a bishop, I ordain candidates to these same orders. Today still, consecrating bread and wine leaves my knees a little weak. My hands have been burning, as if I am carrying burning coals in my palms for so many years now that I cannot imagine it ever being otherwise (it started around the same time that I began to follow the path of ordination). The energy I feel flowing through me during a healing service is impressive and probably has an equally large effect on me, as I hope it does on the person requesting healing.

## New Wine in Old Wine-Sacks

What then went wrong? Or was it right? I suppose the first important point is that truly undergoing the process of Seeking the Light changes the way you think, the way you feel and the way you live. Not that I have now found "the" Light, as I soon came to realise that the Light is not a destination, but a journey. The emphasis lies on seeking it and seeking it is an on-going process. The ramifications of changing my attitude towards life, the universe, etc., spilled over into all aspects of my life. I divorced, remarried, divorced again, and remarried again. Some time between all that I became ill and had to give up my work. A work project that was my livelihood and on which I had spent many years was relegated to the rubbish bin. I went back to University to study clinical psychology, specialising in relationship and family therapy.

In the various spiritual organisations I was involved in I started noticing the discrepancy between what was preached and how the individuals within those organisations dealt with one another. That definitely started getting to me. The first thing one does in such a situation is to try to bring about change. But soon I came to realise that the inertia of an organisation is a pervasive thing— the tendency to avoid change is in-built in all nature, and so it is in people and the organisations in which they serve. One by one I left the organisations—sometimes disillusioned, sometimes the "zing" simply wasn't there anymore.

Then one day it happened. My wife Brigitte and I were sitting in the congregation during a service in Haarlem, the Netherlands, and during the Eucharist I had one of those lucid moments when everything seems to fall into place. Fleeting, but salient and lucid. How this moment would work itself out into nuts and bolts, I did not yet know, but the direction was clear. I should stop trying to change organisations and their functionaries and get down to starting something new. No new wine in old sacks. With very little concrete, I discussed matters with my father, already by then some years retired after his term as Presiding Bishop of the Liberal Catholic Church. The result was my resignation as a priest of the Liberal Catholic Church and my consecration as an independent bishop by the equally independent bishops Johannes van Alphen, Mario Herrera, and Benito Rodriguez on the 4th of June, 2006. This was the beginning of a new phase of my life, a phase in which I ceased to be a follower and gradually started to take responsibility for the insights I had the good fortune to receive.

That is the historical part of my story—no more trying to change what is existing, but setting up something new. I suppose you could say that I changed as well. But what is that something new I am bringing about? What is so different from that which is already being done, to warrant the energy to set up a new thing? In keeping with the principle of Head, Heart, and Hands, I will start by explaining the philosophical aspects of my new approach before telling you about how this translates in practical terms. The philosophical approach in brief has to do with relevancy, authority, responsibility, and unity.

## What is Relevant?

An organisation, in my view, exists in order to facilitate a particular goal. However, the available energy is often usurped by the process of keeping the organisation alive, leaving little for the goal for which the organisation was originally constituted. People become self-important, and power struggles and political gaming take the place of the work itself. The system becomes rigid and replicates itself in such a way that only those willing to tow the line become its new leaders. Many a free-thinking spirit walks away disillusioned, but the system trudges on. In terms of relevancy, to me this means that as it is not possible to do away with the organisation entirely, the energy spent on running the organisation should be pared down to an absolute minimum.

The result is that more energy is freed up for the work itself. This implies, of course, that the work can be properly defined. The adage "if you don't know where you are going, any road will get you there" is certainly applicable. The question I continually ask myself is: Why I am (still) doing what I am doing? To what purpose? Does it give me energy or does it cost me energy? Is the investment worthwhile? I soon came to realise that relevancy in this respect has little to do with what I do on Sunday morning. It has more to do with translating the Sunday morning experience into how I function during every single moment of this earthly existence. Seen from this vantage point the passage in our liturgy "here do we offer unto thee our selves, our souls and bodies as a holy and continual sacrifice unto thee" takes on a very profound meaning: We are the oblations being consecrated during the Eucharist.

## What About Authority?

Perhaps the boldest thing an individual can do is limit his or her authority to matters that concern his or her own experience. It is a well-known principle in clinical practice that you cannot change someone else. People can only change themselves, and will only do that if they want to change. A spiritual teacher claiming authority and attempting to impose his or her way on others will sooner or later be disappointed with his or her followers. *Followers.* If your goal is to enlighten people, how in God's name can you enlighten them if they are *followers*? The idea is paradoxical to the extent that it is unworkable!

Working this idea out a little further: A brain scan of a person looking at an object is almost identical to the brain scan of the same person imagining seeing that same object—to the brain there is no difference between what you actually see and what you imagine you see. So, objects do not give rise to experience, awareness does. Therefore the only surety I have in this life, is that I am aware that I experience. I cannot prove that you, the reader of these words, actually exist. Even if you tell me that you exist and that you too are aware that you experience, how do I know—how can I prove—that this is so and I am not just creating an experience of you telling me this in my own mind? So, if I know that my experience is my reality and I know that what I am experiencing is exactly that—my experience—who am I to tell you what you should be experiencing? Each individual is an authority on his or her own experience. This does not mean we cannot talk about it and share our experiences with one another. Yet the ultimate authority on experience lies with the individual him- or herself.

This means rethinking the role of the spiritual teacher. The priest is not there to play intermediary between the individual and God, or be the authority on matters spiritual, but to help people make their own connection, to empower them. The priest's first and foremost task is to make themselves redundant!

## Whose Responsibility is It?

Interpreting this view on authority as *laissez faire* is complex. It is true that one should let individuals decide for themselves what they are going to do and how they are going to do it. Funnily enough, despite all one's efforts, this is what actually happens anyway. It is false in that it does not mean that the individual is like an isolated island. Others do have a role to play by their influence, due to their interaction. When it comes to responsibility, it is a matter of taking it for your own part in whatever it is that you are busy with—in this case your influence and your part in the interaction. To others we should give the freedom of choice, even if we are of the opinion that by their choice they are making a mistake. By all means give information, but there is a very fine line between giving information and making a judgement.

Placing authority on the individual does not mean that there are no boundaries. Conditions or preconditions to interaction may be imposed, and as long as they are clearly stated up front, they need not be a problem. What it does mean is that having stated realistic conditions and preconditions, no one other that the individual him- or herself is in a position to judge whether or not to make use of the offer that is made. Whether the individual chooses or another imposes, either way the consequences are for the individual, so why not empower the individual by giving them both the choice and the responsibility for that choice?

## What, Then, is the Uniting Factor?

In a nutshell: Diversity. The emphasis shifts from large organisations determining exactly how each "i" should be dotted and every "t" crossed—uniformity—to several small organisations, each working on a project that suits its temperament, culture—whatever.

More importantly, an entirely different definition of the priestly role becomes evident. Doing service at the altar is now the task of a celebrant—an individual who has been ordained to the priesthood and who has been trained to such a degree in ritual functioning that he or she may take the lead in the public celebrations of a particular circle.

Why then, would someone want to become a priest in the Young Rite? The function of the ritual is the symbolic condensation of primordial processes or archetypes into our manifest world. To put it more simply, by enacting a ritual the participants are able to experience the archetypal processes operating in both the universe and the human being. The result is an ever-unfolding insight. By taking an active role and being involved in this symbolic enactment, the experience goes deeper. The gap between the insight and practice in daily life becomes smaller. Which leads to the next subject: Priesthood and the spiritual process is not only about what happens on Sunday. The ritual is a tool with two major objectives—the development of the individual as a result of experiencing the ritual and the outpouring of positive influence upon the world. The second objective is greatly aided by the first: when participants go about their daily activities they also spread the beneficent influence amongst those with whom they interact.

The role of the priest is no longer limited to the performance of ritual and acting as an intermediary. It now becomes that of a spiritual teacher. The lessons learned in the ritual affect the way the individual lives his or her life. It leads to the recognition that awareness of your own inner experience is the best vehicle towards knowledge—or development, even enlightenment, etc. This means that the priest no longer tells people how to lead their lives, but follows Christ's example and lives his or her life according to Christ's pattern. Teaching by example is far more effective than teaching by giving instructions and laying down prohibitions.

So, the path towards the priesthood is open to all. By becoming a priest you deepen your experience of the ritual and become a beacon of beneficent energy. Being a priest in daily life means pouring the Love of Christ out over the world, and living your life so as to best approximate His example. It is expected of candidates for the priesthood that they live a life of integrity that breathes respect for life. A certain lifestyle is recommended. The ordination to the priesthood is an inclusive, developmental path. It does not confer the right, nor impose the duty to publicly celebrate the services of the Young Rite.

Public celebration is no longer the task of a priest, but of a celebrant. For those who wish to become celebrants, the "clean" lifestyle is no longer a recommendation, but a requirement, as is a thorough ritual training. All may become priests in the Young Rite, irrespective of race, colour, creed, sex, sexual orientation or even their membership of, or function in, any other religious or spiritual organisation. Therefore the possibility of being ordained to the priesthood lies within reach of every individual. More importantly, the individual not only has choice, but responsibility. This is empowerment and a substantial step towards a free, universal priesthood—the priesthood of the people.

The ideal to which every circle works is the celebration of the Eucharist where everyone is a priest. Each celebration is like a con-celebration. This does not mean that only those who have received the ordination to the priesthood are welcome in the circle. The ordination process is an awakening of something that is innate. Everyone can potentially access this innate functioning. The ordination process is meant to facilitate the opening of the channel so that this functioning becomes operational. The time to start using this functionality is not dependent on a time scale or progress along the ordination process. It is dependent on the individual's capacity to recognise and access it. Does this raise questions about the Apostolic Succession? Most certainly it does. Hence the decision to insist that at least the one person leading the ceremony be validly ordained within this succession. All participants fulfil their priestly role to the extent that they are willing and able. This is both realistic and makes everyone's efforts valuable.

Another appropriate question is, are the ordinations being "given away?" What if someone only joins a circle to obtain ordination and then leaves to go his or her own way? Is this a form of misuse? Perhaps it is, perhaps it isn't. Near the end of the ordination liturgy, the new priest is commended: Freely hast thou received, give freely. If I give you a gift and you choose to use this gift in a particular way, am I to be judged for the way you choose to use it? If I give you a gift and this gift includes the responsibility to use it according to your best judgement, then I am giving freely. Without this implicit trust the gift would not be a gift, but the mere delegation of a task. Irrespective of the structure of the organisation, there simply is no guarantee that individuals will tow the line—so why require it? By coercing people into submission you implicitly invite devious or defiant behaviour. Those who are just coming to get an ordination will comply as long as it is necessary and subsequently leave anyway. To put it in terms of empowerment, the example set by giving this trust is worth far more than the efforts necessary to control such so-called misuse. Then there is the subject of experimentation. Large organisations generally seek uniformity and this is necessary in order to maintain the "corporate identity." A tradition provides a framework. The content may be filled in by those working according to that tradition. The choice in the Young Rite is for the various circles to each discern their own direction in choosing this content. Experimentation is encouraged. Only by trying various alternatives can one truly distinguish the value of any particular element. As a point of reference and in order to vouchsafe the Apostolic Succession, the traditional form of the Holy Eucharist is maintained and always used for the major ordinations. This traditional form is by-and-large the same as the shorter form of the Holy Eucharist used in the Liberal Catholic Church. Of course, experimenting in several ways only becomes truly interesting if there is a forum for sharing ideas. One of the platforms used by the Young Rite for sharing is the Sophia Circle. The Sophia Circle is a platform open to all bishops who subscribe to an esoteric point of view. All of the bishops of the Young Rite are also members of the Sophia Circle. New ideas therefore spread and are inspired from further away than just the circles working in the Young Rite tradition. This is yet another expression of inclusivity: neither the influx nor the outflux of ideas is limited by proprietary considerations. Practically this means that a lot of material is placed in the public domain—via the internet—for general use.

As to the esoteric orientation of the Young Rite, this is a natural consequence of the philosophical tenets regarding relevancy, authority, responsibility, and unity. A literal interpretation of the scriptures or the Catholic tradition would make this manner of working untenable. Not the letter, but the spirit of the Word is my guideline. Without wishing to devalue the entirety of the scriptures by a single iota, the radical message of Christianity to me can surely be summarised in: "Love thy neighbour as thyself." This is a command in a positive sense. In like spirit the Young Rite attempts to offer possibilities, not organisational rules and regulations.

How do people or groups join the Young Rite? Although no barriers for entry are erected, resources are a limiting factor. Any group, wherever in the world, may adopt the Young Rite way of working. The limiting factors are generally related to finding suitable episcopal support. Often the aid of another independent bishop—for example one of the members of the Sophia Circle—is called in to help get things going.

One of the insights the esoteric tradition has given me is that of cyclicity. A day is born with the rising of the sun, this same sun rises to the meridian and sets in the occident bringing a period of darkness. So also the pattern of manifestation of every thing: A human life, a culture, a tradition, an organisation. Everything is born, grows up, grows old and dies. The old makes way for the new. The Young Rite is not for everyone, not for ever, nor is it complete. It is a work-in-progress and for the time being. There are many paths up the mountain and this is but one. I believe that the summit is the birthright of every individual and the path by which it is reached is unique and valid for each and every one of us.

In conclusion, my path as an independent bishop is a varied one. As a psychologist I may not subscribe to the Rogerian manner of therapy, but I do agree with his general vision regarding the human being: Every individual is seeking self-fulfilment. What I hope to achieve is to inspire. True inspiration frees the mind and lays the emphasis on what you want to do, rather than on what you think you *have* to do. Some people want to be followers and there is absolutely nothing wrong with that. Others want to more fully embrace their own choice, their own responsibility, and their own authority in their lives.

I hope that I have been able to sufficiently convey my conviction that to be free I need to give others that same freedom. *Omnia Vincit Amor.* In Light, Life, and Love, my blessings to all.

The Most Rev.
Kenneth Babauta

Society of Franciscan Workers

# "To Help Those in Most Need"

MY TRUE JOURNEY AS AN independent Catholic really began in November 1995 in Vallejo, California. I was dying from AIDS contracted pneumonia. I came home from the hospital and my family put me into my bed to await my death. I welcomed the inevitable: my lover died several months previously of the same disease. My family gathered one last time around my bed and prayed for me. I was relieved when they finally left the room. I wanted to rest, but much more I wanted the silence. I started to drift off and then, like watching a movie, I saw my entire life literally unwind before me. As I was watching episodes of my life, I realized that these were scenes of things regarding which I felt shame. I was very regretful and sorry about those episodes of my life that I had long forgotten about. As they unfolded I relived them with the same intensity and thoughts. Then an overwhelming sense of guilt and shame came over me and I shouted out, "Jesus, my life was a lie. Please forgive me." Then, from a corner of my view, a tiny speck of dim light caught my attention. I became fixated on it. It started to grow larger and larger. It also became brighter and brighter until the light filled my whole vision. As the light became larger, it also became warmer. Suddenly the light focused itself on me, and as it directed its rays on me I felt the heat become hotter and hotter until I felt like I was burning up. The heat felt like a million needles were piercing my flesh but instead of pain I felt tremendous love. This feeling went through me and around me—it surrounded me completely. My mother's love could not compare with this love—it was so much greater it was overwhelming. The light was so white nothing I have ever experienced can come close to it. My eyes saw through it and it did not hurt watching the light. Then a voice asked me if I helped those who needed it the most. I answered, "No." Then I found myself back in my room wide awake. I had no fever. It was morning and I got up, put my clothes on, and headed for the kitchen.

I found my parents there. They looked like they'd seen a ghost but before they could talk, I asked for a bowl of oatmeal. I did not usually eat oatmeal but something told me to eat oatmeal that morning. My father went to the store and got the oatmeal for me. As I was eating, I realized that they were still staring at me. I had to get this oatmeal down. Before I finished the bowl of oatmeal, I asked for scalloped potatoes. I did not know the name of the kind of potatoes I was asking for so I had to describe it. The strange thing about this is that neither my parents nor I had ever had scalloped potatoes. We are Pacific Islanders and scalloped potatoes are not part of our diet. My sister's mother-in-law baked the potatoes for me and brought it over that afternoon. I felt like I was eating something foreign.

I was already an ordained Old Catholic priest, but I had been too busy working at an oil refinery to devote time to my vocation. Now everything changed. God sent me back to help those in most need. I didn't know exactly what this meant but I had to tell God that I loved Him for the experience of His love and forgiveness. I put a cross above the mantle of the fireplace and I stared at it. I was reliving my God-event and stood there for hours. I proceeded to say mass alone with my mother's dogs laying at my feet. Soon my parents joined me and before I realized it my whole living room was filled with friends and relatives joining in as I faced the altar, saying mass.

The word was out, "Fr. Ken is back from the dead and saying mass the old way." Relatives would visit me asking for prayers and advice. People came to see for themselves that I was still alive. I would look into their eyes not listening to their words as if I was searching for something. Maybe it was the light that I experienced that I was searching for. My mind wasn't thinking. I still felt like I was in a cloud and someone was directing my movements. I couldn't talk long with anyone and I did not have the energy to share my experience with anyone. I would come out to say mass and then go to my room to rest. I ate little. All I wanted was silence and the opportunity to gaze upon the corpus on the cross.

I started St. Victor's church in my living room. There were fifty people at the beginning who regularly came to mass. I never wanted them to come; they just came. There was all sort of talk about what to do, how to go about starting the church, more about the politics of the church but nothing about the truth of God's forgiving love. This couldn't last and it didn't. When I met my partner, Jeffrey, and started to date him, the church began to fall apart. Where I had fifty people, I had only five left. Jeffrey apologized for the fallout but I said that it was OK. I wanted the people to know the truth about me, that I am gay and also a child of God. I believed that God sent me a partner, one that I hadn't found in all the gay bars I'd frequented in the past.

A Mexican lady and her sister came to mass one day and offered her beauty shop for a chapel, and so St. Victor's moved to American Canyon. The congregation grew to sixteen, mostly women and children. We had fiestas to Our Lady of Mt. Carmel and St. Victor. We started processions during the feast days. Baptisms, Communion, and Confirmations were a regular occurrence. Weddings started to be a frequent event in our small parish. But again this was not to last. I take full responsibility for not supervising my parish council properly. I was too trusting of them and took them at their word that they were diligently doing their duties. We were broke, so broke that I had to do weddings to help bail out the church.

We moved out of American Canyon and held mass at people's homes and even in their garages. We finally found a church in which to hold services. We were at a Lutheran church and rented their sanctuary for mass. We were there for over a year. Then we move to our present location in a Christian Church (Disciples of Christ), and we have been there for over five years. St. Victor's has an HIV/AIDS men's group which meets on Wednesdays. The congregation has grown to fifty members with sixteen regular communicants on Saturdays. There is a clergy team of three priests. The parish is part of the Society of Franciscan Workers under the auspices of Bishop River Damien Sims.

Now a Bishop for quite a few years, I've been guardian of St. Victor's for thirteen years altogether. It felt like it was only yesterday that we began. I also volunteer as pastor of a small Disciples church in Richmond, California, and have been doing this for four years. I am still searching for the meaning of the question posed to me by the light: Am I helping those in most need? Maybe the answer isn't as important as the question, because I have found that as long as the question is fresh in my mind, my life's work is never enough and never finished. Amen.

Mar Alexei (Rt. Rev.
Alistair Bate CCP, MADiv)

Titular Bishop of Hebron,
Liberal Catholic Aposolic Church

# "Writing Straight with Crooked Lines"

I AM A BISHOP OF THE Liberal Catholic Apostolic Church, a member of an independent Passionist community, and also of the Independent Liberal Catholic Fellowship. In this short piece I'd like to share with the reader how I came to be who and what I am and to reflect with you on some aspects of my journey, believing that however unconventional our path may be, there are are many paths up the same mountain. I believe that God delights in the diversity of His creation and the diverse paths we may take to reach Him, so we can all benefit from sharing our insights. In my own case, maybe sharing my own rather odd story can help others to avoid some of the pitfalls I experienced!

It is often said that God writes straight with crooked lines. In terms of my own life and particularly my vocation this has proved to be very true, but it is not something I regret—rather I rejoice in it, for the circuitous route to my present vocation as an independent bishop has been full of interesting people and places without which my life would certainly have been the poorer.

I was born in 1964 and brought up in a reasonably devout Irish Anglican household where the prayer books lived in a designated space on a shelf in my mother's bedroom near to her extensive collection of Sunday hats. Yes, those were the days when ladies still wore hats to church and no one seriously considered ditching the 1662 *Book of Common Prayer* altogether! I had to learn the prayer book catechism by heart at school—it did me no harm at all—and in due course I was confirmed. I had and still have a great love of Cranmerian English and happily now, as a Bishop of the Liberal Catholic Apostolic Church, I use our own lovely liturgy "services of Love and Blessing" along with the Liberal Catholic Liturgy, both of which have preserved much of Cranmer's style while expunging any excessive preoccupation with sin. However, I still indulge in a little 1662 *Book of Common Prayer* occasionally and particularly when I'm officiating at Healing Services. On these occasions I often use Cranmer's beautiful words at the distribution of Holy Communion:

> "The Body of Our Lord Jesus Christ, which was given for thee, preserve thy body and soul unto everlasting life. Take and eat this in remembrance that Christ died for thee and feed on Him in thy heart by faith, with thanksgiving."

This beautiful invitation was etched in my heart, particularly in my mid-teens, when having extricated myself from a brief entanglement with some Pentecostals, I started serving a week day Holy Eucharist at St. Patrick's

Cathedral, Dublin. The words "feed on Him in thy heart by faith with thanksgiving" now speak to me more clearly than ever, not only of the necessity of nurturing the spirit through a faith-full passion for Christ, but also of the great value of an "attitude of gratitude," something which attracts to us a multitude of graces and blessings.

As a teenager my spirit was nurtured not only by frequent communion but also by the friendship of a holy priest. Canon Bradley, Dean's Vicar and generous host, was known to many of us High Church boys simply as "Father" and cut a rather picturesque figure around St. Patrick's Close in his cassock, cape, and wide-brimmed hat—which he found on holiday in Spain. He was hugely influential in my young life, a good man, though also quite obviously very human. I wished to be just like him, only even more "Anglo-Catholic," of course!

Around the same time I started some volunteer gardening for the Community of St. John the Evangelist, a few of the last remaining sisters of an Anglican Order in Dublin. Known to my mother's generation as "the Protestant Nuns" the CSJE were considered an oddity in the Church of Ireland, but nevertheless admired for their exquisite embroidery which adorns many an otherwise dreary Victorian Gothic Protestant edifice out in the middle of a field! Then, through the "Protestant nuns," I met my first "Protestant monk," an Anglican Franciscan from Belfast who was down in Dublin for a mission. I immediately determined that his Community was the path for me, that is until I discovered the other ten Anglican communities and determined to check out most of them. I wrote to several and generally got encouraging letters back though naturally most communities even in the early 1980s were not too keen on taking a postulant straight from school.

Now why, the reader might legitimately ask, would an eighteen-year-old wish to enter a monastery with a view to staying for life? Well, twenty five years on I haven't got to the bottom of that question, though I suspect that it was a mixture of a genuine divine call, an active romantic imagination, and an insecurity born of a sense of rejection by those closest to me. In the long run this mixed motivation has all been grist for the mill as my true vocation steadily unfolds.

Arriving at Alton Abbey in the beautiful Hampshire countryside on a warm summer's afternoon in 1982 I fell in love with the place straight away and at my first service in the Abbey Church—Solemn Vespers and Benediction—I knew that this was a place I would feel right at home. I had, of course, read a great deal about monastic spirituality and history by this point. However, I had no idea I was as immature as I undoubtedly was. Being a well brought-up boy I was a punctual and devout novice, if a little woolly on the sacrifices inherent in the life. On reflection, I think I was really seeking a family and above all a close relationship, and a monastery is not the right place to seek either! When eventually I decided to leave, my Novice Master, a wise old monk said "Well, Brother, if there's one thing we've done for you, it's to teach you that you're not St. Therese!" St. Therese had been my daily companion and guide for many years and I had somewhat naively imagined that I could ignore the the deep sense of loneliness I felt, "offer it up," and then die "in the odour of sanctity" at the age of twenty four, just like St. Therese! I was wrong. However, most of my two years in monastic life were happy and were certainly very formative—the Benedictine tradition has, for example, given me a huge appreciation for the daily Mass and Divine Office and this daily liturgy is still pivotal to my vocation as an independent bishop, which in my case has both pastoral and contemplative dimensions.

The purely contemplative vocation is a rare one in the Church and I was perhaps a bit arrogant to think that it could be mine, simply because I felt a strong attraction to it. A cloistered life was not to be, but I have, by the grace of God, ended up with something close and perhaps for me a bit more grounded. I think I would have been a rather self-obsessed monk and self-obsession will drive a monk mad. It is providential therefore that God, knowing my weaknesses, has given me a mainly apostolic vocation instead. My busy urban ministry in Edinburgh offering weddings, funerals, and other rites of passage takes me out of myself and encourages empathy. Funerals, in particular—which are my daily bread—constantly confront me with the realities of life, death, grief, and pain, and I am glad of these constant sobering facts of life. The Eucharistic Heart of Jesus burns with an infinite compassion for all the people to whom I'm ministering and so I am called to bring a Passionist Heart into these pastoral situations. At this point I'd like to share with you a short piece which inspires my community and I, called "A Passionist Heart." It really sums up my Passionist ideals, particularly concerning the apostolate:

> "A life-giving gift, our Charism—experiencing the Passion of Jesus—draws us into the Heart of God. It enables us to be who we are, and is the foundation of all that we do. For it is by entering into the pain and suffering of Jesus that we are

strengthened to enter into our pain and suffering, and so we are able to stand with others in
theirs. Although the Passion of Jesus offers no
hope without the Resurrection, this Resurrection
Hope cannot be experienced unless first we are
willing to stay with the suffering. When God is
discovered in the ordinariness of life, the
Charism and inspiration given to St. Paul of the
Cross remain alive. The Spirituality flowing from
the Charism enables us to enter into relation-
ships that may not otherwise be humanly possible. It thus creates and is sustained by a sense of
community and expresses itself in empathy,
depth of prayer, down to earthness and a willingness to be vulnerable" (The Passionists—
Australia, New Zealand and Papua New Guinea,
2003).

As well as the Passionists, another great monastic influence on the development of my own particular life style
and ministry has been Blessed Charles de Foucauld and
the Little Brothers of Jesus. They have taught me that one
doesn't need to live in a monastery to be a monk and that
to bring the Eucharistic presence of Christ to a council
estate in Edinburgh is a potentially valuable vocation in
itself. If I did nothing else but offer a daily Mass for the the
needs of the Church and the world, I would consider my
vocation fulfilled and I know of many other independent
priests and bishops for whom the essence of their vocation is to offer Mass for particular intentions. Many mainstream clergy find it hard to understand our simple and
some would say "medieval" confidence in the efficacy of
the Eucharistic sacrifice and perhaps this is just one of the

many unfortunate consequences of church modernisation and reform.

However, to get back to the story—on leaving the Abbey I hadn't the first clue what I was going to do and did some volunteer work with handicapped children for a while. As I had become used to the Novus Ordo Mass in the Abbey I thought it was about time I became a Roman Catholic. It turned out to be a big mistake, although I did meet some wonderful people. In fact, I was befriended by both a Carthusian monk and a Redemptoristine nun— both very rare species nowadays!—and I'm convinced that both of them were living saints. Still, I found Roman Catholicism, as a whole, too repressive and culturally alien, and consequently I didn't settle there. Undoubtedly one of the big issues was, of course, the thorny issue of sexuality. Despite my traditionalism, I've always been "out and proud" and I simply could not take the required degree of self-oppression under which gay men labour in the Roman church.

At this point my spiritual odyssey took a quirky turn. I was working with people with learning difficulties as a carer and one of my colleagues was a Spiritualist who encouraged me to attend a meeting with her. Now, my own father, though a practising Anglican, was also a convinced Spiritualist and to some extent I was brought up with a knowledge and acceptance of the movement, so going to a meeting was not such a big step to take. It is a step I have never regretted and along with monasticism I would say spiritualism has played a key role in my spiritual development. It was not long before I was sitting in circles for the development of mediumship and enjoying some success as a medium and healer. Since that time the world of spirit has never been very far away and being a spiritualist—with a small "s"—is a significant factor in enabling me to sustain a ministry which is most often focused on providing for the recently departed and their bereaved relatives and friends.

By the time I first got involved in organised Spiritualism I was living in London and in that great city I did a variety of jobs, including administration for *Psychic News*, the weekly Spiritualist newspaper. After that, I worked as an administrator in the HIV/AIDS field for a few years. I attended Spiritualist meetings, Quaker meetings and would also regularly attend an Anglican Mass usually at a monastic house rather than a parish.

Back in the monastery I had once read an essay by Dame Maria Boulding, OSB, entitled, "A Tapestry from the wrong side," in which she suggests that God is making a tapestry picture of our lives and on the right side he can see quite clearly the beautiful picture that is emerging whilst from our perspective we see only the tangled threads, knots, and loose ends. Well, after eight years in London, leading (it has be admitted) a rather fun-filled life and sowing quite a crop of wild oats, I needed a glimpse of the tapestry from the right side and needed to re-find God badly. The problem was that like so many spiritual seekers my spirituality was now so eclectic it was hard to see where I might possibly fit in. Then I discovered the Shakers and after a couple of years of letter writing and a visit to the only remaining Shaker community in the world, I was off to Maine, and a great adventure it was!

The Shakers, for those who may not be aware of their history, are a communal church of Brothers and Sisters who profess three key principles: Celibacy, Confession, and Community. While I did not find the family I sought in the Benedictine monastery, I certainly did in the Shaker community which is even called "the family." I wove baskets and fed sheep for a couple of years, loved so much about the community life and distinctive Shaker spirituality with its matter-of-fact attitude to spirit communication, its openness to the Divine Feminine, its joyful worship and its focus on gratitude, humility, and love. I even found that celibacy isn't so scary after all! Therefore, it is a great sadness to me that Shakerism does not enjoy wider appeal than it does presently, as it has so much to offer. I was now in my mid thirties and seemingly out of nowhere I was bitten by the study bug! I hadn't had a university education and all of a sudden I had a huge appetite for learning. Now, a Shaker community, with a distinct preference for manual work is not the place to be bitten by the study bug—"Hands to work and Hearts to God," Mother Ann Lee said. So once more I said my goodbyes and came back to Britain to begin my university education, a Masters degree in Divinity at the University of Edinburgh.

My university career was a tremendously enjoyable four years. I ended up with a good deal of knowledge and my faith journey had taken a few interesting twists and turns. After my first year at University I joined the Order of Bards, Ovates, and Druids and was also attending the Unitarian Church which, largely due to a wise and laid-back minister, provided a welcome contemplative space in my busy week. After graduation I continued my association with the Unitarians and for a couple of years worked as a Lay Leader in two different congregations—in fact I still minister occasionally to the Newcastle-upon-Tyne Unitarian congregation and I will always be grateful to the Unitarians for the pastoral skills I gained whilst working with them. Undoubtedly, for a few years I was a Unitarian in every sense, perhaps the result of my Trinitarian faith having been whittled away by exposure to good modern biblical criticism and uninspiring Protestant theology at University. Loss of faith is something I would heartily recommend as a temporary measure, as I believe that a static faith is no faith at all. A stable faith, on the other hand, is something to value. In my younger days my belief in doctrines, such as the Trinity, was a simple intellectual assent, based on ignorance of the cultural context in which the doctrines developed. Biblical studies undermined my ignorance and taught me that these beliefs were houses built on sand. They needed to be knocked down and the house of faith built on the solid rock of personal apprehension of the mysteries, even if this apprehension does not very well lend itself to rational description. I suppose I am an old fashioned liberal who perhaps owes more to Schleiermacher than an orthodox Catholic should. Take this quote for example, which neatly sums up my position with regard to doctrines and dogma:

> "Religion...is neither a metaphysic, nor a morality, but above all and essentially an intuition and a feeling.... Dogmas are not, properly speaking, part of religion: rather it is that they are derived from it. Religion is the miracle of direct relationship with the infinite; and dogmas are the reflection of this miracle" (Quoted in Kedourie, Elie; *Nationalism*, p. 26; Praeger University Series, 1961).

Doctrines and dogmas are of central importance to me, but as mysteries to be lived in and pondered over rather than facts of dubious historical veracity to which I must give assent.

So, having existed in a theological limbo for some years, with little to sustain me of any real substance, all of a sudden my faith in the central mysteries of Christianity was restored. It was pure intuition and feeling and felt like a gift of grace from a transcendent source, a mystical experience very hard to describe. I simply woke up one morning and there it was, the gift of faith. I hope never to take this gift for granted again.

Having rediscovered the central doctrines of Christianity in a fresh way and having learnt some years earlier of the existence of the Independent Sacramental Movement I then determined that to seek ordination from an "Indie" bishop would be the best way forward. As confirmation of my call within a few weeks of my decision a friend introduced me to his neighbour, +Michael, an Independent Bishop with many years experience of the movement. We soon became friends and within the space of a few months I was ordained deacon and then priest.

The most wonderful thing about being made a deacon was, of course, to have the Blessed Sacrament reserved in my home for Eucharistic adoration, and naturally my first Mass as a priest was also very special. Some mainstream clergy will of course find it quite shocking that the Blessed Sacrament should be reserved at a living room altar. I prefer to think that I have an Oratory-cum-living-room rather than the reverse. I expect that in the pre-Constantinian church the sacrament was reserved in private homes and perhaps too in the one room cells of monastic hermits. Sharing a flat with the maker of heaven and earth in his Eucharistic form is certainly an incentive to mindfulness!

Naturally, as an "Indie" I do not have the luxury of a clerical stipend and actually live as one of the poor, among the poor, in a council flat, but I subsist quite happily on what I earn from ministry—mostly funerals, a couple of hundred of them each year in fact! As long as I have my home altar I'm happy and last year, happily, my vocation developed further when Bishop Michael, Brother David, and I established the Companions of the Cross and Passion, committing to live as much as possible by the Passionist charism. I was elected to the episcopate by my community and the Bishops of the Independent Liberal Catholic Fellowship, of which we are a part. Since its foundation CCP has lost one member, for whom the lure of traditionalist Catholicism was too strong, and gained three more members, good candidates; one a former Mormon missionary, another a former member of an RC religious order and one already an Indie priest. We feel very blessed. We have recently started a regular monthly public Sunday Mass in central Edinburgh at which we can minister to a larger group than would be possible in our home oratories and I am happy to say that the work goes from strength to strength.

I still have a great interest in things Celtic and teach courses occasionally in Celtic Reiki, Celtic spirituality, and the Druid tradition, and lead a small but thriving Celtic worship group called the Trinity Grove which meets monthly.

On being consecrated a bishop I found, somewhat to my surprise, a new devotion to the apostles themselves. Knowing that the multiple lines of apostolic succession which I have received can be traced right back through the eastern and oriental churches as well as the western church has given me a renewed sense of connection with these ordinary but heroic men who passed on to us the great grace of faith in Christ.

Looking back on my first inklings of vocation, when I had thought that I might be a Church of Ireland Rector and then an Anglican monk, I never would have chosen to be part of the Independent movement, even if I had known about it, but now that this is where I find myself I feel a deep sense of security and certainty that this is where God has wanted me to end up all along. Our Lord said "I have other sheep who are not of this flock" and it is now my privilege to live the gospel as best I can as a quite marginal cleric ministering to those who are, for the most part, similarly marginal or marginalised. Altogether, I am very thankful for a full and rewarding if unconventional ministry.

Back in the days of my Anglican Benedictine novitiate I was given a prayer card by a visiting Blessed Sacrament Brother which read: "God knows he loves he cares, nothing this truth can dim. He gives the very best to those who leave the choice to him." Of course I didn't leave the choice to God, but scampered after one dream after another, yet somehow God managed to direct my wild wilfulness. I can truly identify with Cardinal Newman's well known words:

> "I was not ever thus, nor prayed that Thou, shoulds't lead me on. I loved to choose and see my path, but now lead thou me on, I loved the garish day and spite of fears, pride ruled my will remember not past years."

But God can use even pride to land us where we ought to be, as the Shakers say:

> "Tis the gift to be simple,
> tis the gift to be free
> Tis the gift to come down,
> Where we ought to be."

The one thing that I have learnt is that God does not compel. The place where we ought to be is not some round hole into which I, as a square peg, am compelled to fit. The true vocation is to be oneself and to realise that, as Emmet Fox writes: "the Will of God for us is always something joyous and interesting and vital, and much better than anything we could think of for ourselves."

The big challenge, now as ever, is to really be present in each day, to take time with Mass and Offices, to make space for reflection, to be still and trust in God, not only for myself but for our whole world. My hope for the future is now to do as Dr. Rowan Williams advises, to strive for that degree of release from self that prayer becomes "letting God be himself in and for us" (Williams, Rowan, *Tokens of Trust*, Canterbury Press 2007, p.157).

The Most Rev. Jonathan Blake,
BA Hons., Dip. PS

Presiding Archbishop of
the Open Episcopal Church, UK

# "Pioneering a Religious Revolution"

I WAS BORN A NATURAL IDEALIST with an inherent sense of the Divine and a desire to champion the oppressed. These fledgling aspirations were nurtured in a mixed faith Christian/Jewish home, although my parents' interfaith marriage meant the family was ostracised from the Jewish community. I was baptised at the age of eight.

Cast into public school education and longing for home, I found solace in the chapel and was confirmed.

An unexpected invitation to assist at a summer camp after A levels brought me into close contact with evangelical Christianity for the first time. I surrendered my life to Christ and felt an immediate vocation to the priesthood.

I decided to read Theology instead of Law at University, and my life was consumed with the quest to understand how best to be a servant of God.

Durham University introduced me to the Charismatic movement, and the sense of the immanently powerful intervening God. Miracles and the extraordinary were to be expected, and brave ventures were met with unexpected resources.

My idealism found expression in a rigorously applied frugality: I believed that Christian solidarity with the poor required abstinence and simplicity of lifestyle. It was a path resonant of St. Francis: eccentric and pugnacious.

In addition I smuggled Bibles, medicines, and vital supplies to Christians behind the iron curtain, worked as a Samaritan, established a "Third World Shop" in my college, which is still trading, supported Amnesty International's letter writing campaign and tried obsessively to fill every idle moment with Christian ministry.

Having attended a Boarding School with an Anglican foundation, and having been baptised at the local parish church, it was inevitable I would explore my vocation through the Church of England.

I was accepted for post graduate theological and pastoral training at St. John's in Nottingham but delayed for a year to put my idealism to the test. I graduated, worked again in Eastern Europe, and then hitchhiked to Calcutta to work with Mother Theresa's Missionaries of Charity. My time in India matured me. I was confronted by a world of abject poverty and amoral desperation in which religion was used as a commodity.

It was a year of extremes. I waded through contaminated flood water chest-high to bring aid to the homeless, distributed relief supplies for Operation Mobilisation, helped Tear Fund with their rehabilitation center project, nursed the sick in Mother Theresa's Home for the Dying, and rescued children from the streets. Having arrived a frugal student in jeans and sandals, I adopted the attire of the poor and went about barefoot. I returned to England stripped of my Western pretensions, determined to try to reconstruct a more integrated view of the world and a relevant faith.

Life at theological college appeared trite after such a year. The dogmatism of the evangelical mind was claustrophobic, and the extravagant claims of the charismatic seemed illusory. I arrived angry and left angrier, eager for ministry but unsettled as to my true Christian identity.

I was ordained deacon in 1980 and priest in 1981, and went on to serve in the Church of England for twelve years.

I relished the breadth of parochial ministry but grew to resent the autocratic rule of the Incumbents and the corruption and compromise inherent in institutionalism. I shuffled a pack of radical and controversial beliefs and approaches, pushing at the boundaries and challenging the status quo, in an attempt to disturb and express my discontent with the complacency and self-righteousness of the church.

The fact I was no stranger to controversy reflected also an inner ambivalence to how I could best fulfil my vocation.

I was stimulated intellectually by my tutor, a university chaplain with liberal views, and experientially by my involvement with the World Conference on Religion and Peace, an interfaith peace and justice NGO attached to the United Nations. I was elected to their international executive board and travelled widely, initiating projects and attending meetings. I organised a Peace Bus, taking fifty young people from different faiths, cultures, and countries, from London to Moscow through Eastern Europe before the fall of the iron curtain, offering prayers on the way at places of immense significance such as Auschwitz and Bergen-Belsen.

I was increasingly nudged towards the potential within Christianity to find a mandate to promote a universal and truly catholic worldview.

I helped build up a depleted congregation in South East London into a thriving church. We raised over a quarter of a million pounds to fund a vital remedial and expansion project providing additional facilities for the community while also supporting many charities. But I also used my position to challenge the status quo. I stood alongside the ambulance staff during their strike in 1992, was arrested during non-violent Gulf War protests for writing a biblical quotation on the external walls of the Houses of Parliament, and celebrated the mass in sack cloth and ashes. I preached that God was more likely to be encountered outside the church walls in the poor, lost, and needy rather than at our comfortable weekly worship; that our receipt of the sacrament of true communion was fulfilled in everyday life, not through bread and wine alone. It wasn't what many wanted to hear.

The limitations of working within the Church of England left me disillusioned. I felt I was servicing an elitist group within society, at the behest of church authorities who demanded that I should bolster numbers to increase revenue and the Anglican profile.

The details of my departure from the Church of England and my launch as a priest working independently of denominational structures are included in my book, *For God's Sake Don't Go To Church*, published in 1997.

It had become clear to me that the call to priesthood had nothing to do with being part of a religious multinational, rather being called to incarnate God's Word in every way possible and every situation to which one was called. This required flexibility, ingenuity, minimal structures, few material responsibilities and a willingness to embrace the breadth of our Christian, religious, philosophical, and cultural heritage.

I nailed my 95 Theses to the door of Canterbury Cathedral, setting out what I saw as the challenges facing the Church, for which I was arrested but not charged.

For the five years after 1994, I pioneered the provision of an apostolic itinerant and inclusive ministry in the United Kingdom, providing the sacraments of the church to individuals and families in their homes and centers of the community.

Decades of protectionist practices by Church of England parishes had denied many families access to the sacraments, so this new provision met with widespread interest and requests for ministry. The need was great, and I co-launched the Society for Independent Christian Ministry ( SICM ) on January 1st, 2000, to provide a structure to facilitate, ordain, and oversee ministers working outside the traditional denominations.

In December 2000, I was ordained priest and consecrated a Bishop within the Old Catholic Succession. In 2003, with two other Bishops, I issued the Hazlewood Declaration inaugurating the Open Episcopal Church (OEC), an inclusive Catholic church, governed by Bishops, following Canonical Rules, able to confer Holy Orders, drawing upon the theology of the Old Catholic mother church of the Netherlands rather than later developments, expressing a Trinitarian faith and working ecumenically, inter-denominationally, and inter-religiously.

The vision of the Church was rooted in an understanding of the resurrection covenant requiring a manifestation of the life of God in community with no walls or divisions, but united in Christ.

The Canons of the Church are orthodox and radical. They root the belief of the church in the Creeds and early Councils but they interpret the practice of the church in ways relevant to modern understanding and insight.

We practice an open altar, welcoming all to receive, be they babe, child, or aged; Christian, other faith, or seeker; believer, agnostic, or atheist. No one is excluded from those who gather at our Eucharistic celebrations. We see applicants for ordination not as men or women, gay or straight, able or differently abled, but simply as people. We regard all those who aspire after the good to be companion pilgrims on the divine path. We do not require obedience, stifle debate, or enforce belief. We are hungry for God, passionate in service, devoted to ministry.

While observing form and liturgy in the transmission of Holy Orders, we are eclectic generally in worship and in church life. We are not a club carving out a specialised culture, rather the world in its totality is our resource to encounter God.

Since its inception, the Open Episcopal Church has experienced challenge and change, but it is committed to high standards, integrity, and sincerity. It has no interest in building its own empire, nor in promoting any particular brand of Christianity, rather being a living organ within the body of Christ, infused with the Holy Spirit, and yearning to embrace and share, in true catholicity, the entire world as one family.

The media have shown an interest in my independent

ministry from the outset. I have appeared on numerous documentary-style and chat-style TV shows, including two appearances on *Richard and Judy*, have been featured both in the quality and tabloid press, and have taken part in various radio broadcasts.

Part of this interest has been generated by the social revolution that has been underway within and alongside my ministry.

The legislation for flexibility in the provision of secular weddings was emerging at the time I launched independently, and what the law enabled at the state level, I began to offer within the world of religion, following what I entitled "the continental method." Couples would carry out the legalities for marriage in a registry office with just a small number of witnesses, and then I would provide the full sacramental marriage service wherever they wished.

Weddings have taken place all around the world in people's gardens, stately homes, forests, beaches, hill tops, aeroplane, castles, football grounds, theatres, an early Saxon settlement, speedboats, apple orchards, stone circles, pubs, clubs, and even underwater.

Such unusual settings for sacramental and other ministry compared to the traditional stereotypes have intrigued others. Whereas in the past it was only royalty or the wealthy who could arrange a baptism suited to them, from the first "home baptism" I conducted, as reported in *The Times* in 1994, suddenly this facility was available for everyone.

Since then, tens of thousands of people have gathered in people's homes and other venues across the United Kingdom to celebrate the sacrament of baptism. Even on the summit of Mount Snowdon, in a circus ring, at a night club, and in a Wild West Bar.

Even in bereavement, creative presentation can offer comfort; expressing the culture and needs of those involved. I have taken a funeral in a garden situated beside a lake and another in the intimacy of a front room. I have been present while mourners danced and sung in tears beside the coffin. I have seen ashes sifted through the mourners' fingers

The celebration of the God who is everywhere must also find expression at the heart of our worship. The Mass has been celebrated in Trafalgar square, with the breadth of communicants embracing commuters, tourists, the street homeless, and the prostitutes of Soho.

The practical application of faith has also been a vital part of ministry. We have taken the homeless and refugees into our home, and helped to rehabilitate addicts of drugs and alcohol.

The media were also fascinated when I became the first cleric to advertise my willingness to conduct gay weddings in the gay media. The provision of legitimate religious ceremonies for the gay community across the country formed part of the groundswell that led to the change in legislation introducing Civil Partnerships.

On February 14th, 2001, I conducted a gay wedding on *Richard and Judy*'s morning TV show. It proved groundbreaking television, and was inevitably controversial. *The Daily Mail* published critical articles about me and my Episcopal orders that the High Court agreed could have been regarded as defamatory.

It was not something I could ignore, as it called into question my status and integrity as a Bishop and the validity of my Orders. Over two years of litigation followed which concluded positively for me in that it upheld my integrity and my Episcopal status. Associated Newspapers International had to bear their costs, which amounted to well over £100,000, and a proportion of mine. It was a significant victory and an important one for the Church.

Much of my time now, as the presently elected Archbishop of the church, is devoted to archiepiscopal duties. However, my personal ministry is considerable and, to give some idea of its scope, past and present, I will outline some statistics.

In the years since my launch as an independent minister, I have travelled across England and to fourteen other countries. Over 150,000 people have attended my services, and I have nearly 10,000 people on my address files for whom I have provided ministry. I have welcomed nearly 2000 people into the life of the church through Holy Baptism.

It is thus clear that I am not interested nor involved in some "hole in the cupboard" style of ministry for its own sake. I received a call from Christ to give my life in service to God and, while recognising my faults and failings, that is what I have sought to do and continue to do. I know that the good news of God's love transforms people's lives, the redeeming work of Christ offers the grace of forgiveness and new life and the sanctifying work of the Holy Spirit empowers both individuals and communities to share in the Divine work of establishing God's order within our hearts and world. That is my calling.

The light that has guided me and maintained a buoyant and eager faith is my intolerance of insincerity. The multiple compromises required in denominational ministry lead often to inertia and disillusionment and yet the carefully constructed employment package makes it almost impossible for a free-thinking cleric to escape. I thank God that I did and to this day remain fulfilled and vibrant in my priesthood and episcopate. SICM and the OEC enabled me to ensure that the path to freedom I had discovered would be available to others.

The main denominations have not reacted happily to these developments. As with all emergent churches we have been misreported, maligned, and resisted. In the early days, Anglican Bishops campaigned to have our adverts removed from the *Church Times.*

Later, Anglican and Roman Catholic Bishops campaigned to try to prevent us being able to consecrate the first Catholic woman bishop in the Open Episcopal Church, the Rev. Mother Professor Elizabeth Bridget Augustine Stuart SSB, MA, DPhil, in the Chapel of Royal Holloway & Bedford New College, University of London, Egham, Surrey. Thankfully, the Chaplaincy and the University held firm in permitting the service.

We are in negotiation with Churches Together in Britain and Ireland to achieve membership, but have so far found that such organsiations can close ranks too easily to exclude applicant churches without justification even by their own criteria.

We have so much to offer a tired and fragmenting church which must reinvent itself if it is to survive in our rapidly changing world. Stuart Murray, in *Church After Christendom*, Eddie Gibbs and Ryan Bolger in *Emerging Churches,* and Pete Ward in *Liquid Church* have begun to research and write about present day experiments in Christian community and church life. Our own contribution to this movement is similarly being researched.

We want to move away from the insularity and self-seeking nature of what Christendom has often become. We are the itinerant church encouraging spirituality within naturally formed communities of family and friends. We encourage home-based Christian education and worship. We identify God's work and God's ministers without and within the denominations. We look to enable individuals to practice their priesthood formally throughout the everyday and the everywhere. We believe in the true church, without walls, which consists of hearts within which the Spirit of God is at work.

There *is* a loneliness to working in this manner, but only the loneliness known by our Lord, the apostles, missionaries, and martys and all those who have sought to be true to the path of Christ, often encountering misunderstanding and ostracisation.

Within this, the spiritual wells from which I draw refreshment are the Mass, Daily Office, the Scriptures, the writings of the Saints, the untidy holiness of domesticity, my wife and five children, and those to whom I have the privilege to minister and who minister to me.

Following the tradition of those such as Gregory of Nazianzus, I regard my home as a church, and have converted the top floor into a beautiful Chapel. There is also an altar in the kitchen.

As a family, we pray and worship together and regularly celebrate the Eucharist. I encourage the children to pray and even informally to consecrate the elements. The presence of God, the blessed sacrament, the sense of the numinous and the Divine is the foundation of everything in my life and home, yet not in a heavy-handed way but with that deft touch that one hopes holds the balance of mystery and the familiarity of intimacy.

I celebrate the festivals of the Church publicly. At Christmas, the house is so festooned with lights, at the heart of which gleams a lifesize Nativity, that hundreds come from miles around to see and make donations—amounting now to nearly a £1000 a year—to charities working with the poor. At Easter, a life size bloodied crucifix hangs from the front of the house which is transformed into the risen Christ on Easter Sunday. We observe the ancient Holy Week and Easter liturgies to the full, kindling a blazing bonfire before dawn to herald the coming of the Light of the World. Colored helium balloons bearing messages of love, faith, and hope are released at Pentecost; fireworks ignited at Ascension.

Everyone around knows of "the Jesus house," including the hundreds of school children who file past each day on their way to the five local schools.

When I come across denominational Christianity in the many churches dotted around the area, it reminds me of that which motivates my independent ministry. I want to ensure that the treasures of Christ and the inheritance of the saints are not stolen by professional religion to be cloistered away in church and chapel, where they end up working towards the opposite of their intention.

Our detractors look to criticise this apparently new way of operating. They say that no Christian can be independent and a church without laity is a mockery. My reply is that our church has a wider lay base *pro rata* than many of the denominational churches. I take services for over 200 people every week and they are not the same group repetitively attending, but new hearts encountering the Gospel, new seeds being sown. I remain in contact with a credible proportion of those for whom I have provided ministry, being asked for further spiritual help as their lives unfold. I also offer a daily Mass and Divine Office for those who want to join in congregational worship and offer to link families to receiving local churches if we do not have a local congregation.

Independence, too, is a misnomer. No christian is independent. As part of the body of Christ, we are organically connected. Personally and within the OEC we look for every opportunity of cooperating with other Christians. It is not we who create isolation, but those whose approach has created schism and hatred throughout history, who remain exclusive to this day as to which orders may be respected and who may receive Communion.

From an analytical perspective, the OEC is part of a cyclical and well observed tradition which involves grass root communities and smaller churches experimenting, pioneering, and ultimately refreshing the mainstream denominations with their experience. Already, aspects of ministry which I and the OEC have practiced are being adopted by others, and I predict more will be adopted in the future, whether it takes decades or centuries.

Whether my ministry, the OEC, the independent Catholic movement or any earthly form of ministry survives matters little, as long as the Holy Spirit continues to confound every human attempt at entrapment with mischievous and extraordinary grace, and leads our stubborn hearts to God.

The Most Rev.
Timothy W. Michael Cravens

Independent Catholic
Christian Church

# "From Baptist to Bishop"

I COME FROM AN ECCLESIASTICALLY checkered
background. My father and eight of his brothers were
ministers in various conservative evangelical Christian
denominations. My father started out Free-Will Baptist,
was for a short while a Cumberland Presbyterian minister,
and spent most of his career as a Southern Baptist minister except for a few very unfortunate years during my
childhood when he pastored a couple of Assemblies of
God congregations. My uncles served as ministers in the
Nazarene, United Methodist, Cumberland Presbyterian,
Presbyterian Church USA, and Free-Will Baptist denominations.

An only child, I was baptized at the age of 5 by my
father in a Southern Baptist church, very early for a
Baptist. We were members of the Assemblies of God from
the time I was 6 until I was 9, when we returned to the
Southern Baptist fold. During this period, my father

befriended an Episcopal priest, and I attended a service in his parish and was fascinated by the liturgy. I requested a *Book of Common Prayer*, and the priest gave me an old 1928 prayerbook, as they were using the transitional books that led to the 1979 revision. Shortly after, I found a dead bird in the yard, and ran to get the book and read the Burial Office over it, with my dog Sofia in attendance. One of my favorite games to play thereafter was giving a large green plastic Porky the Pig funerals, with a purple and white towel draped over it as a flag, as if he had been a state dignitary. I also baptized all of our kittens. I later got my parents to let me plan the Advent family devotions with an Advent wreath, something shockingly high-church for our family.

The summer I was 10, I was elected as a messenger (as Southern Baptists call their delegates) to the Southern Baptist Convention from our church (my parents were the other two messengers). A couple of years later, my father left the Southern Baptists again, for non-denominational charismatic churches, and was unemployed for 5 years. We would go to one church for a few months, until my father invented a reason why the pastor was scripturally unsound, and then we would go to another. Around this time, I developed a hobby of reading about various denominations and writing to their headquarters for literature. I even read about the Polish National Catholic Church and various Old Catholic churches and obtained some literature about them. At one point, we started going to a United Methodist church, and I joined when I was 15. A year later, in 1983, I served as a youth lay delegate to the Holston Annual Conference of the United Methodist Church. One of the painful aspects of this experience was that I had begun to come to terms with being gay, and the Annual Conference voted overwhelmingly to demand that the General Conference ban the ordination of "self-avowed, practising homosexuals." I skipped that session, and increasingly began to recognize that I could not have a home in that denomination.

## Discovery of Liturgical and Eucharistic Christianity

In my senior year of high school, I started attending the Episcopal Church, and was confirmed as a freshman in college. I had longed for weekly Eucharist, and was very happy to find it in the Episcopal Church, as well as to discover the riches of the liturgy. I found that the Eucharist enabled me to experience God's presence in my life in a tangible way that I never had before. I began to say Compline, and soon added Morning and Evening Prayer.

While in college, I majored in Judaic studies, with a minor in Hebrew. I began the process toward ordination in the Episcopal Church, but withdrew because I did not feel that I would be able to go through the process in a Southern diocese as an openly gay man. I decided to go to Harvard Divinity School on my own. I had some negative experiences in an Episcopal parish in Boston that, while welcoming LGBT people fully (they were one of the first parishes in the Episcopal Church to bless same-sex couples) and celebrating the liturgy very beautifully in the Anglo-Catholic tradition, was in other ways extraordinarily dysfunctional. I gave up hopes for the priesthood and began attending the traditional Latin Mass in a Roman Catholic parish, and was ultimately received into that denomination shortly before graduation.

Although I had given up on the idea of becoming a

priest, the yearning came back, and after working for a few years, I entered the Franciscan Friars of the Atonement at Graymoor. After a year and a half, I realized that I could not become a Roman Catholic priest in good conscience, because of their exclusion of women from ordination and LGBT folk from ecclesial life, and I left both the Friars and the Roman church to return to the Episcopal Church. Although I had hopes once again of pursuing the Episcopal priesthood, I was turned down, probably because of my less-than-traditional ecclesiastical journey and my strong advocacy for marriage equality for same-sex couples, an issue that is quite controversial in Anglican circles.

## Joining the Independent Catholic Movement

Shortly after leaving the Friars, I met John Plummer, who gave me my first in-depth introduction to the Independent Catholic movement, which I soon embraced, and he ordained me and ultimately consecrated me a bishop (of the Mission Episcopate of St. Michael and St. Timothy), while I continued to attend my local Episcopal parish. I had developed a confessional statement in preparation for consecration that described my approach to the Christian faith:

1. We accept the Holy Scriptures of the Old and New Testaments as the rule and ultimate standard of faith, containing all things necessary to salvation, being interpreted in the light of the tradition of the Church, human reason, and the experience of the people of God. We hold those books known as apocryphal or deuterocanonical in high regard and leave to individual conscience the question of their inclusion in the canon.

2. We accept the Apostles' Creed as our Baptismal Symbol and the Nicene Creed as the sufficient statement of the Christian faith. We hold the Athanasian Creed in high regard for its teaching on the doctrines of the Trinity and the Incarnation.

3. We celebrate our faith and are sustained through the Sacraments, the outward signs of inward grace. We accept the two Sacraments ordained by Christ Himself—Baptism and the Eucharist—ministered with unfailing use of Christ's words of Institution and of the elements ordained by Him. We also accept the Sacraments of Confirmation, Ordination, Marriage, Reconciliation, and the Anointing of the Sick.

4. We accept the Historic Episcopate, Priesthood, and Diaconate, locally adapted in the methods of administration to the varying needs of the nations and peoples called of God into the Unity of the Church.

5. We believe in the inclusiveness of the Gospel and offer the Church's ministry of the Word and the Sacraments to all regardless of race, ethnicity, ability, sex, gender, sexual orientation, or economic or social status. In particular, we believe that Ordination is open to all qualified candidates regardless of sex or sexual orientation and that Marriage is open to all couples who make a solemn covenant to commit their lives to one another regardless of the sex or gender makeup of the couple.

6. We believe in the Ten Commandments and the Summary of the Law as the standard of morality for Christians.

7. We believe in the daily Christian life of prayer, which receives its highest expression in the Lord's Prayer.

To compose this confessional statement, I combined

the four areas of the Roman Catechism (Creed, Sacraments, Ten Commandments, and Lord's Prayer) with the Anglican Chicago-Lambeth Quadrilateral and added the statement on inclusion. Essentially, my vision as a bishop has always been to adhere to Christian orthodoxy, in particular the doctrines of the Trinity, the Incarnation, and the Atonement; to carefully preserve the seven sacraments and apostolic succession; and to recognize the equality of women and LGBT folk in the life of the church.

At first, my ministry was a hidden ministry of liturgical prayer in intercession for the world, offering the Eucharist alone in my studio apartment in Peekskill and reading the office in the "chapel of Our Lady of Metro North," as I sometimes referred to the commuter train I took to work each weekday. I had one priest in my care, who lived first in Oregon and then in Texas.

A year into my episcopate, John Plummer and I joined a small independent Catholic jurisdiction which, a year later, proved to be unsatisfactory, and on December 12, 2002, we formed the Provisional Independent Catholic Christian Church (we dropped the word "provisional" six months later, when it became apparent that we wouldn't be joining another jurisdiction). We adopted this Statement of Faith, adapted from the first confessional statement:

The Independent Catholic Christian Church and its member ministries and individuals accept the following principles:

1. The Old and New Testaments as our Scriptures

2. The Nicene Creed as the sufficient statement of Christian faith

3. The seven sacraments of Baptism, Eucharist,

Confirmation, Marriage, Anointing of the Sick, Reconciliation, and Ordination

4. The historic threefold ministry of Bishops, Priests, and Deacons in the apostolic succession

5. The ordination of both male and female and both gay and straight Christians as Bishops, Priests, and Deacons and the marriage of both same-sex and opposite-sex couples as sacramentally valid

6. The Ten Commandments and the Summary of the Law as the standard of Christian morality

7. The Christian life of prayer, expressed in its highest form in the Lord's Prayer

In 2005, I moved to Philadelphia, where I met Fr. Joseph Menna, the founder and prior general of the Augustinians of the Immaculate Heart of Mary (AIHM). The order had started the St. Mary of Grace parish, and I was privileged to attend the parish from its first public mass, held a couple of weeks after Fr. Joseph's ordination. The order was at that time affiliated with another jurisdiction, but several months later, they felt that the Independent Catholic Christian Church would be a better fit, and transferred. Shortly thereafter, John Plummer resigned from the jurisdiction, as his ministry was moving in a different direction, although we remain friends. The collaboration between the ICCC and the AIHM transformed my ministry, because whereas before, it had been eremitical, carried out mostly in private, now it became very public and community-oriented. The AIHMs have always emphasized community, with a practice of going "from table to table," moving from the celebration of the Eucharist to sharing a meal in common. This community aspect of the ministry has greatly enriched my experience of the Independent Catholic movement.

## Foundations of Independent Catholic Life

In my ten years' experience in our Independent Catholic movement, I have seen a lot. Based on those observations, I have concluded that there are several elements necessary to nurture one's vocation as an Independent Catholic Christian and ensure an authentic spirituality.

A. *Sound Doctrine*. Christianity is the religion of Jesus Christ, and before all things it is an absolute necessity that we recognize who Jesus Christ is and what he has accomplished for us. We believe in the One Triune God and in God's self-revelation in the person of Jesus Christ, who is both fully God and fully human. Through His atoning death and resurrection, Christ won for us victory over sin and death, which we receive as we are united to Christ in His death and resurrection both in our baptism and in our daily life. We are strengthened in our understanding of these basic Christian mysteries by frequent reading and meditation on the Scriptures, most especially the four gospels, and we are rooted in the 2,000 year tradition of the church (ecumenically understood). Isolation from the mainstream of Christianity is dangerous.

B. *Lively Prayer Life*. Next, it is very important that every Independent Catholic Christian, and most especially those called to a religious, diaconal, or priestly vocation (and let's face it, that's most of us!), develop a thriving life of prayer and communion with God. Without significant time devoted to communion with Christ on a daily basis, we risk allowing our lives as Independent Christians either to wither into nothingness or else be distorted into a hobby. Anyone who has been around the movement for any length of time has run into those who love to go to ordinations and other such events and wear all the pretty vestments (not that there's anything wrong with pretty vestments—I have closets full of them!) but who spend no time in prayer apart from these infrequent gatherings. In the King James Version of the Bible, Jesus' admonition in Matthew 6 reads as a commandment to "enter into thy closet, and when thou hast shut thy door, pray to thy Father which is in secret," and we should do this daily— and who better than an Independent Catholic can take some icons, some fabric and some discarded old furniture, and transform a closet into a fabulous chapel?

I find that the spiritual source of everything I do lies in my daily celebration of the Eucharist ("I will go unto the altar of God, even unto the God of my joy and gladness") and the Divine Office, particularly in praying the Psalms, meditating on Scripture, and honoring the Incarnation with the daily recitation of the Benedictus, Magnificat, and Nunc Dimittis. We Independent Catholics are in a unique position to be intimate with the liturgy, and I hope that all who are called to our way of life will nurture that intimacy.

*C. Comfort with Solitude.* Although there are some pretty wonderful Independent Catholic communities around, the reality for most of our people is that much of our spiritual lives must be conducted in solitude. And only when we can come to embrace that solitude, that exile, can we fully live out our calling and vocation as Independent Catholic Christians. For years, I only rarely celebrated the Eucharist with a community, instead offering it each day in solitude. And it can become lonely and discouraging. But only if we are willing to live with that loneliness and discouragement, can we know the Lord's blessing on our lives.

Even for those of us blessed to be part of a strong local community, there can be a sense of isolation from the larger churches, many of whom may not see our ministries as "real." I have seen a lot of time wasted and a lot of misguided efforts diverting energy from what is needed in the vain attempt to get Rome, Canterbury, Utrecht, or other mainstream churches to "recognize" us and "take us seriously." Enough! If God sees our efforts and knows what we are about, we should be satisfied. And if not, then all the recognition from all the mainstream churches in the world cannot make up for that lack. We need to be faithful to the calling we have received from Christ, and leave the results up to God, who looks not on the outward appearance, but on the heart.

There are many in our movement who are unstable or worse. Indeed, there are many unstable people in every religious movement, but the decentralized nature of our movement gives them much freer rein to flourish and cause trouble. In reaction, some in our movement would like to see a centralized structure to weed out the problems. Of course, this will never happen, and it ignores the fact that the chaos stems from the great freedom of our movement, which allowed us to consecrate a female bishop six decades before the Episcopal Church did, and to open our doors to the LGBT community as early as 1946, long before any other churches. The healthiest response to the problems in our movement is to be found in Jesus' parable of the wheat and the tares—rather than attempting to weed out the tares and thus risk losing some of the wheat, we should focus instead on our own growth, our own spiritual lives, our own communities, and leave the problem people alone—not letting them upset our own local communities, but not worrying about what they do on their own.

*D. Authentic Community.* Although authentic community is rare in our movement, it is a vital component of a genuine Christian spiritual life. Some are called to an eremitical ministry in solitude—and because this vocation is so little understood in most mainstream churches, we have a unique role to play in nurturing it. However, even those with a solitary vocation should be a part of a larger community, to which they can be accountable and from which they can receive support for their hidden vocation. Many others are called to participation in the small, close-knit families that our movement provides. Most mainstream parishes offer a model of ministry in which there is a paid staff of clergy and perhaps professional laypeople who provide much of the ministry, with the laity often being fairly passive (outside of a small group of highly involved volunteers). This model certainly meets the needs of many Christians, and I don't mean to criticize it. However, for others, we can provide a model of a small base community in which every member plays (or at least has the opportunity to play) a fairly involved role in making the community work. Without paid clergy, we have the opportunity to ordain all those who demonstrate a valid call, without worrying about whether or not we have the resources to pay them. We can offer laity an opportunity to take a very active, responsible role in their own spirituality. One lay member of our parish in Philadelphia has observed that she has learned more about the Catholic Christian faith in her year with us that in all of her years in the Roman Catholic denomination. Rather than bemoan our small numbers or lack of paid clergy or buildings, I think we should celebrate our unique contribution to the Christian church and focus on how we can complement what mainstream denominations offer, rather than attempting to replicate it.

To be sure, authentic community is difficult, and requires a great amount of hard work and dedication. It is no picnic. There will be those who are attracted to it who seek to benefit from what it has to offer (or from their unrealistic perceptions of what it ought to offer) without contributing—or worse, engaging in destructive behavior. And some of the work of the bishop is to protect the community from such people—acting in charity for all, but not exercising a misguided mushiness. I sometimes joke that my consecrators did not engage in full disclosure because they forgot to tell me that there is a lightning rod hidden in the mitre. But, at the end of the day, community is worth all of the struggles and aggravations it requires, when one encounters the growth in the grace of our Lord Jesus Christ that results.

*E. Inclusiveness/ministry to those on the margins.* We have a long history of ministering to those on the margins. In 1929, long before Anglicans began ordaining and consecrating women, Izabel Wilucka was consecrated a bishop for the Old Catholic Mariavite Church of Poland. The last bishop consecrated by Rene Vilatte before his death was George Alexander McGuire, consecrated for the African Orthodox Church, empowering African American Christians at a time when they were excluded from full participation by the Roman and Anglican denominations. George Hyde opened the doors to the gay community in 1946, and Michael Itkin was advocating for gay equality in the 1960's as an independent bishop, long before Gene

Robinson or even Troy Perry. Jesus hung out with a pretty unpopular crowd, and was criticized for it by the religious authorities of his day. In our vocation as followers of Christ, we are called to be at the margins. We will never receive the recognition that others do—nor should we, for that would hinder our ability to minister to those at the margins. We are called to a thankless, hidden calling of ministering to those that larger churches cannot or will not reach. Rather than worrying about money, recognition, numbers, or buildings, we should be concerned with how faithfully we are living out God's call to minister to the one lost sheep, and let our Anglican, Orthodox, Protestant, and Roman sisters and brothers shepherd the 99 who are safely in the fold. They have a different call, and we should rejoice that God has given to all of us our place in Christ's church.

*F. Sense of Humor.* Finally, there is one gift that every Independent Catholic Christian *must* have to survive, and that is the gift of humor. There is much that is hilarious about our movement—even some of the things that are holy—and only if we can see and laugh at the holy hilarity of our churches can we serve the Lord with gladness. Our beautiful vestments (bought on sale or sewn on our sewing machines) are meaningful symbols of service— and the pictures we take of ourselves wearing them are ever so slightly ridiculous at the same time. It's okay to laugh at ourselves! May we always be blessed with the gift of laughter from our God who wipes away every tear.

## Conclusion

Would I have chosen this vocation freely at an earlier age? Probably not. But God has richly blessed me, and given me companions on the journey. I hope and pray that our ministries may continue to receive the rich blessings of God as we prepare ourselves for that great day when we shall be united with all whom Christ has redeemed at the heavenly banquet, to enjoy communion with the Triune God for eternity.

The Most Rev.
Richard Alston Gundrey

Presiding Archbishop Emeritus,
Catholic Apostolic
Church of Antioch

# "Seeing the Christ in All Life"

I AM HONORED TO HAVE BEEN ASKED to share my story and connection to the independent Catholic movement. As of this writing in June, 2009, I am Presiding Archbishop Emeritus for the world-wide independent Catholic Apostolic Church of Antioch with headquarters currently located in Phoenix, AZ, USA. Currently we have 75 clergy in good standing and 33 registered churches within the USA.

I started studying in 1985 directly under our founder, Patriarch Herman Adrian Spruit. My studies took two and a half years. I was ordained a priest by Patriarch Herman on October 31st, 1987, at his headquarters in Mountain View, California, USA. I have been active within our church and the Independent Catholic movement for more the twenty years.

Let me respond to the question: "What prompted you to get involved in the Independent Sacramental

Movement?" The background is that I was born September 20th, 1934, baptized and raised in the high Episcopal church in the Flushing area of Queens, New York, where I was exposed to sacramental worship. I was a boy soprano choir member, eventually an altar server and was also involved in youth activities.

During my marriage and the birth of my two children I attended the Episcopal Church sporadically. After my divorce in 1972 when I was looking for more answers in my life I found a local unit of the United Church of Religious Science in Santa Fe, New Mexico, where I had been living since 1967. This opened up for me a new dimension to spirituality. Ideas such as the power of our consciousness, meditation, taking responsibility for my life, getting away from dogmatic teachings, rules, and regulations attracted me. At that time, the teachings of Ernest Holmes, the Founder of Religious Science, as expressed through his ministers and practitioners, really spoke to me. I needed that information at that time in my life. It helped me take control of my life when prior to that I was unconscious and did not know I could set my own direction. I was with Religious Science for 14 years and was a Religious Science practitioner for 10 of those 14 years. I had a good understanding of what I call contemporary metaphysics. The organization encouraged me to become a Minister under their flag but at that time this would have required moving to Los Angeles for three years to go to ministry school. I had made up my mind at that point that I wanted to be a minister of some type and wanted to do spiritual healing work, which I was doing as a practitioner and at which I was very successful. However, I was not willing to leave Santa Fe, which I loved then and deeply love now as my spiritual home. I seemed to know at that point that I wanted to commit to spiritual work or start a group here in Santa Fe. I did not want to take the luck of the draw at some church located anywhere else in the USA.

It was in 1985, on the Plaza in Santa Fe, that I ran into an old friend, Dean Berenz, known to me from the contemporary metaphysical community. I asked him what he had been doing recently. He said "I have just been ordained into a metaphysical Catholic Church." Those were buzz words for me. I came to realize that the sacraments were embedded in my consciousness and a part of my being. I sensed from Dean that this "Church of Antioch" that he was talking about allowed the freedom to bring metaphysical, mystical, and esoteric ideas into sacramental worship and rituals. Religious Science is not a sacramental church and this sounded right up my alley. To make a long story short I contacted Herman and Meri Spruit and took a personal trip to California to meet them. I found them a very sincere couple trying to grow an independent Catholic church that allowed freedom of conscience and choice as well as freedom of interpretation of scripture. The church was an open and inclusive church having its doors, altars, and Holy Orders open to all humanity regardless of who or what you are.

To answer the question directly, what got me into the independent Catholic movement was being allowed to teach and use my metaphysics within sacramental rites and worship. This was the perfect combination and home for me.

Have I been fulfilled? Immensely. I never would have devoted twenty years to this movement if I were not completely happy and spirit-filled with my ministry.

"How did my sense of calling manifest itself?" It just seemed to become evident to me as I studied and learned things spiritual over time. I did *not* get a flash awakening one night. I think my past lifetimes help me to feel very comfortable and at peace with myself when I function as a priest. It all seems to be very natural for me and I find this work very satisfying.

My current spiritual practice is full-time church work, saying mass and performing weddings and baptisms, generally running the day-to-day operations of our local church. I am completely fulfilled by my celebration of the Holy Eucharist and conducting weddings and baptisms. Nothing can give me a more sacred experience then assisting people to participate in these events.

The Church of Antioch at Santa Fe is our cathedral parish. For the past fifteen years we have rented the world famous Loretto Chapel with its miraculous spiral staircase, which Roman Catholic legend says was built by St. Joseph himself. We have a staff of three clergy; myself, my associate pastor, Bishop Daniel Dangaran who is a former Roman Catholic Jesuit priest, and a staff priest, Rev. Mother Carol Calvert. Average Sunday attendance is 45 to 55 people.

"What have been the pitfalls of the independent Catholic movement?" Of course, credibility. In talking about this issue I must share my experience of twenty years in this movement. Each bishop or priest attempting to do spiritual work in a local area must earn their credibility one step at a time, one day at a time *within their local area*.

We must all act, speak, and live with the greatest honesty and integrity in everything we do. We cannot be concerned about what others think about us. Do *not* bad-mouth other groups, no matter what your opinions of them are. Stay away from the ego attitude of clericalism. We must be very clear about who we are and confident in our own authority and credibility as we do our work. Other will see who and what we are eventually. We earn our credibility one day at a time within our own communities.

Ways this can be done is to first join a local ministerial alliance and get to know the other denominational priests and ministers in your area. Check your egos at the door when you hook up with a group like this. They are trying to serve the same community that you want to serve. You must work together. No one is higher or lower.

Through my local group I was asked to say opening prayers several days every year at our state senate and house of representatives when our state Legislature is in session. This is a great way for people to know who you are. Attend interfaith meetings and events at other churches of various denominations. Get yourself in front of political as well as spiritual leaders in your area.

Financially, most of us are worker priests. We work in the world to support our churches, our families, and ourselves. Yes of course it is our goal, if we choose to run a local church, to have it grow to the point where it can support us financially. This takes hard work, consistency, and spiritual strength. To be a successful independent Catholic clergy-person takes deep dedication and love of this work, to serve God and the people around us without any idea of getting anything back. We will be rewarded ten-fold, spiritually, in returned love and appreciation. In my case I have developed a large local wedding ministry. The extra income from these weddings helps greatly in support of our local church.

Another pitfall of the independent Catholic movement is that we need better seminaries. So many of our bishops train people one-on-one over time, without a standard curriculum. There is so much variance in what Bishops offer and expect of their trainees. I support this great variance according to the theological tastes of the individual churches but there needs to be more standardization within each group. We must get away from renegade bishops making priests or Bishops of their friends, for a fee or even for nothing. We each must have our own integrity to dispense Holy Orders to really qualified people and get rid of simony.

The independent Catholic movement has a lot to offer the world. We provide an alternative but valid sacramental service for those who have been rejected by other churches. We offer worship and theological experiences that many may feel more in alignment with people than in their traditional church homes. Often we offer freedom from certain canon laws and policies that are restrictive. I feel that most, though not all, independent Catholic churches offer freedom of conscience, self responsibility, and freedom of interpretation of sacred writings.

It is our job to make the independent Catholic movement as responsible and as ethical as it can be in our day and age. The independent Catholic movement will only grow and expand to serve all of humanity as the presence of the Holy Spirit moves creatively through each one of us.

# The Rt. Rev. Aristide Havlicek

## The Liberal Catholic Church in Slovenia, Young Rite

# "Amor Vincit Omnia"

IT WAS AN EARLY AUTUMN morning in 1975 and I was the only visitor in a small chapel, high in the mountains, attending a celebration of Mass, for the first time in my life. The old priest was kneeling in front of the altar; the space overwhelmed with the silence of prayer. Astonished as a little child, I was observing and looking forward to what was about to happen....

There was nobody else besides the two of us in that small mountain chapel. The old priest was the father of my friend, who invited me to visit their estate in the mountains above Celje. The priest—Father Konrad—was at that time the only "LCC" priest in Slovenia and one of two LCC priests in whole of Yugoslavia. In his secular life he used to be a decorator, whilst in his his spiritual life, besides being an "LCC" priest, he was also one of the oldest members of the Theosophical Society in Yugoslavia.

I had also become a member of the Theosophical

Society in order to begin serving humanity based on theosophical values. I made this decision mostly because of my spiritual teacher Ivan, a shoe maker from Ljubljana, who spent many years reading and translating H.P. Blavatsky's *Secret Doctrine* into our native, Slovenian language.

As young boys and girls, eager to discover the mysteries of life we used to gather around Ivan throughout our youth. Who am I, where do I come from, where am I going, why am I?? Ivan was helping us to discover these questions; he was guiding us towards and along the sacred path of our mystical education. "*Gnoti seauton*"—discover yourself and you shall discover God. That was his motto. Ivan taught me the correct sitting position, breath control, placing the mind at a point of my spiritual eye (the *ajna chakra*). He showed me the way to go deep inside, to become who I truly am.

In 1979 Ivan left his physical body. Before going to the other side, he showed me how to discover who we truly are by applying the technique he had been teaching me for years and revealed the name of the technique, Kriya Yoga.

Ivan also introduced me to "France," a Slovenian who lived in Australia and had been coming home once a year. France was an amazing expert in Hindu Tantra. Since I was particularly interested in this subject I became his Tantric disciple. Almost unknowingly, Ivan was teaching me Kriya Yoga and France a spiritual relationship towards Mother of the World, the Goddess and the Tantric techniques, Dakshinachare and Vamachare Tantra.

Father Konrad turned towards me and gave me my first blessing: "May the Lord be with you...." I simply observed, and standing in front of me I saw Father Konrad, completely transformed. Instead of a modest smiling decorator who I had met the day before, I saw a man filled with radiating energy. His eyes were not filled with laughter, but with power. I had never seen it before and it was that moment that changed my point of view— from innocent, childlike astonishment I turned inwards, to the state of complete awareness.

Similar to the strange stillness just before the storm... complete stillness of something...I was attending the celebration...observing the body language of Father Konrad and listening to his words. Although I was hearing it and seeing it for the first time, it all seemed very familiar. I remember Father Konrad holding the Host in his hands and inviting me to receive communion. He said: "It is your free will to accept or to reject the gift of God..." Without any doubt I decided to kneel, received the host, and promptly passed out. A couple of minutes later, having recovered, Father Konrad had a mysterious smile on his face. He asked how I felt, so I told him about my experience.

After receiving the Holy Host everything changed. I was standing outside, in the meadow, in a meditative state, facing the hill in front of the chapel. Suddenly a White Lady flew towards me, dressed in white with golden-white hair. Her face, full of grace, revealed deep wisdom and the air was filled with unusual peace. The white lady bent down towards me and caressed my forehead. It was that moment I suddenly woke up. I was back in the chapel; Father Konrad was kneeling beside me. We carried on with the celebration as if nothing has happened.

First thing next morning, when coming back to

Ljubljana, I rushed to my spiritual teacher and told him about my experience. Absorbed in thought, he stood up and went to his room. He came back with a notebook in his hands, where he described an experience he had at the same place, many years ago. He had met the White Lady...at the same place, at a different time but it was the same experience. Ivan had given the White Lady a name: "Mother of the World."

From that moment on I started encouraging all my friends—who were interested in the esoteric and were close to Christianity—to follow the path of priesthood in the Liberal Catholic Church. I encouraged them to become priests, to celebrate the mass, which I thought to be very important for the spiritual development of every individual and for humanity. There was no response to my proposals.

In 1977 I was sent to do civil service in the Bosnian mountains. One of the tasks we all had to share was guard duty. I still remember that long night with a clear sky, *the moon shining over the sky,* and stillness, interrupted only by animal sounds.

Sitting down, I was thinking of my beloved people, when suddenly I was overwhelmed by a strong feeling of love in my chest. The feeling grew and spread all over my body. I began to tremble with the surprise of a completely unknown vibration. This feeling started spreading all over the place. It seemed as if the whole of the moonlight came down to earth, surrounding me. I was in a peaceful state, feeling astonished with the experience. Suddenly there she was—the White Lady. This time I managed to stay present longer than before. I was admiring her face, full of grace and love for everything there is. Even today

I'm still not sure whether I was simply dreaming or if I really did have a mystical experience.

The fact is, the next day I received permission to go home on holiday, which I had found impossible to arrange beforehand, and this gave me a chance to attend a Summer School of Theosophical Society. That year (1978) we were hosting John B.S. Coats, the international president of the TS, and I had a chance to discuss with him my point of view concerning Theosophical work. At the same time I was also able to spent time with Ivan, who joined the Summer School that year. While observing John during his lectures, noticing his altering presence towards others, I had a wish to become like him in my actions. That was the day I made the decision to become a Liberal Catholic priest.

After almost three years of service I returned home. I shared my decision with Bishop Rudolf Hammer whom I had met for the first time when he came to visit us. He was celebrating his mass next to Opatija (Croatia)—a farm estate on the mountain called Ucka and happily both Bishop Rudolf and Father Konrad were very pleased with my decision. On that day, four members of the TS decided to follow the path towards the LCC priesthood. So it began—the journey through the minor ordinations, performed by Bishop Rudolf Hammer. I was getting ready to become a priest under Bishop Rudolf's guidance and visited him in Austria many times, finally becoming a priest in 1982.

The ordination took place at St. Michael's LCC chapel in Zagreb. Never in my life will I forget that moment. The little chapel was full of LCC members from Croatia and members of the Theosophical Society. I was lying on the floor; Bishop Rudolf was reading...when suddenly I caught his look—the eyes of Maitreya—of Christ, the same as in the image which is present in many Liberal Catholic Churches above the altar. This time it was not merely an image—he appeared in all his glory and beauty. I was no longer lying in the chapel. I was kneeling in front of him in a wonderful grove; we were surrounded by white swans. He was sitting on a rock under a beautiful ancient tree. He was not alone. There were many of them, some of whom I knew from before, some of them unknown to me. This vision lasted for a moment, after that I was again aware of being present in the chapel. After our ordination the other three fellow ordinands shared with me their similar experiences. It was this experience that kept on inspiring me during my future years of priestly activities.

However, that same year—1982—I was forced to resign from the Theosophical Society and I registered the LCC with my friends in Slovenia. Every Sunday I celebrated Mass in my room, at home, where my parents used to live. Both my mother and father were very tolerant towards my spiritual activities. Many times my room was full of friends who came to celebrate the mass. In the year 1986, we started our first public appearance under the name "Spiritual Family" which is still active today. We started with monthly public meetings—Full Moon meditations, which used to attract a gathering of up to 200 guests. They were the first public gatherings of the New Age Movement in Slovenia.

The gatherings were organized by our group—LCC Slovenia. We've also assisted other spiritual groups to present themselves to the public in the same way. In that period of radical change we've also shared our point of view and understanding of Christianity through our lectures. At first we started celebrating our masses in hotel halls, then later on we rented a large room, where we carried on with the Celebrations, twice a month, for our friends.

Most importantly for us, was to share our views on Christianity, encouraging liberal Christian theology and a liberal understanding of church history. The only dogma we had was not to accept any dogma, as we believed that dogmas prevent freedom of research and the discovery of subjective truth. It was in those early days that Bishop Rudolf suggested to me that I might become a bishop and, in a way, take responsibility for Slovenia. I decided to do so. The decision was made and it came to pass on March 2nd in 2008.

According to tradition, I was consecrated by three bishops; +Johannes van Alphen, +Markus van Alphen and +Alistair Bate. The consecration took place in Celje, a Slovenian city, where eighty years ago the Theosophical movement and the LCC started their activities. In just the same way as in 1982, I was again lying prostrate on the floor and expected the vision of Him, the one who is the Master of all Masters. Nothing happened...suddenly I felt someone caressing my hair, he was kneeling beside me, wearing jeans, a white shirt with an open collar, laughing gracefully. As suddenly as the vision appeared, so suddenly it was gone. The memory remained, as did a feeling of deep devotion to Him, to his work. With my consecration as a bishop new doors leading towards the path of new responsibility and deep devotion have opened.

Motto—the message of my life's work is *Amor vincit*

*omnia.* I want to remind us all that the strongest and most powerful tool in the entire world is the power of *unconditional love*, which can embrace both light and darkness together in union, and transform them both in the *one and only truth*.

Above all I want to remind people about the importance of the female aspect—the importance of Goddess—great mother of our world, the One who is omnipresent, and to offer the significant teaching of a proper attitude towards the Goddess. How utterly important it is to be aware and to see the sacredness in everything and every being, especially in every female being.

"We are," in the words of St. Peter, "looking forward to a new heaven and a new earth" (2 Peter 3:13). We have a foretaste in this world of the new creation to come. That new creation is not only the redemption of matter, but also the redemption of *time*.

Mar Joannes
The Most Rev. John Kersey, DD

Archbishop of Great Britain,
The Apostolic Episcopal Church

# "On the Path Towards Unity"

I CANNOT REMEMBER A TIME when I was not aware of the presence of God or when I did not enjoy a personal relationship with Him. I have always believed that He had a plan, in which He would use my life as a means, however modest, of fulfilling His will. In return, I have placed my trust in God from the outset, and although the path has not always been straightforward, He has never deserted me and through His grace has shown me further glories of His creation that have allowed me to progress to such a point of understanding as is His will that I should be admitted to. If I were to sum up that progress, it is towards an increasing appreciation of the unity of creation and of the role of humankind within its design.

As a child I spoke frequently to God and began to experience the first of a continuing series of visions of His presence. I was even then sure that these visions were not mere *chimerae* since their essence was understood intuitively by me to be directly that of the Holy Spirit in all-powerful goodness. I did not always understand the full meaning of what I was shown then, and indeed now there are still some things that rightly remain Mysteries. I was also convinced that their nature was of private revelation, and was not intended for wider discussion and disclosure at that time. But of this I was certain; just as I had earnestly pledged my spirit to God at that early age, so God was responding through His manifestation of experiences and opportunities in my life that, were I but to have the courage and the necessary intent, would fulfil His plan for my life and ensure that it was of worthwhile benefit to others.

I was baptised in the Church of England; my parents, although both brought up in the Christian faith, were free-thinkers, and so did not compel religious observance or prescribe belief. Nevertheless, through my schooling and the more important private study that accompanied it, I became aware of the transcendence at the heart of the Christian experience, and the capacity of that transcendence to effect profound change and to form a cogent philosophy of religion. It was a transcendence that I was myself given the gift to experience at that time through playing and listening to music and reading and writing poetry and fiction of various kinds. Later, I would also come to appreciate fine art, particularly the Pre-Raphaelites and the Golden Age of literary illustration.

Through the process of self-education, I became powerfully drawn to the aesthetics of the Victorian era and to the moral and spiritual values that enjoyed their particular ascendancy between the 1890s and the outbreak of the First World War. This was a time of great freedom and exploration, when the Oxford Movement was leading the charge to restore timeless beauty as central to religious experience.

These precepts have remained with me since, and although in some respects my outlook is of necessity forward-looking and progressive, I continue to be strongly influenced by an active awareness of the past and by a sensibility that is to some extent independent of current trends and fashions. In particular, I remain very strongly conscious of the values of the England of my childhood, and of my close family, many of whom have since passed on. I am not concerned with recapturing the past, but with ensuring that we discriminate appropriately in our appreciation of its legacy, and preserve that which is of lasting spiritual value.

At the age of sixteen, I experienced the deaths of four family members—three of whom I had been particularly close to—within twelve months, and although at the time I put on an outwardly brave face, in retrospect I believe I was more affected by this than I perhaps appeared to be. I began to seek the answers to profound questions, and ultimately to look to the mainstream churches to provide these. Later that year, I took up the post of organist at a Methodist church in the locality, and there was confirmed and received Holy Communion for the first time. I was also studying piano and organ at the Royal College of Music then, and was particularly drawn to the Romantic and Gothic traditions in my choices of repertoire; traditions in which the metaphysical becomes of the essence of argument.

Although I enjoyed my association with the Methodists, I soon realised that I was drawn to a form of

Christian expression that left rather more room for the holy mysteries. I read Chesterton, Waugh, Belloc and other writers who described the Catholic life with eloquence, but could not reconcile the considerable attractions of their world with that of the post-Vatican II modernist Roman Catholic Church, nor with my own liberalism on such points as the ordination of women and homosexuality. Yet, at the back of my mind, I wondered if such a faith as those writers had described still existed, and if there was a means whereby what I saw as the natural connexion between traditional sacramental celebration and liberal principle could be realised.

Some while after this, I began to think seriously of a vocation for the first time, and at one point became interested in the monastic life, though soon realising that I was not at that stage suited for the cloister. In my musical calling I was fortunate to work alongside some outstanding clergy, initially the Rev. Dorothy Lloyd-Williams and later, upon taking up positions in the Church of England, Rev. Barry Oakley and Fr. Ken Evans. I observed their work at close hand, learned more about the nature of the ordained ministry, and continued to develop my reading in private study. From all of these elements I learned that discernment was not a matter to be hurried, and that if and when the time was right, God would present the appropriate opportunity to me.

On several occasions I met the impressive figure of the late Brian Masters, the buskin-wearing Bishop of Edmonton, whose Anglo-Catholic influence drew me once more towards a deeper exploration of the Roman tradition. Had I but known it, of course, he was one of us—in Apostolic Succession from none other than Prince-

Archbishop Rudolph de Landas Berghes of the North American Old Roman Catholic Church. Bishop Masters had a wonderful sense of humor and an ability to cut through the splendor of proceedings with an, "It's all so grand here!" Yet he also exhorted us to be close to Christ, and provided an example of this through being completely and unaffectedly himself. Like his Savior, he was always on the side of the downtrodden and the underdog, as happy at the bar of his local pub as in the church. "Never appear for the prosecution" was one of his sayings, and it was advice that I have taken seriously ever since.

I could not reconcile my conscience and liberal beliefs with the dogmatic teachings of the Roman Catholic Church *in toto*, but even then I was aware that the nature of Catholicism was not truly the preserve of a single denomination. At this time, I began to describe my own spiritual path to others as Catholic and to encounter Catholic writers such as Thomas Merton who seemed to echo my own feelings about the individual and the wider Church. Bishop Masters had granted dispensations for some of his parishes to use the Roman *Novus Ordo* at Mass, and I joined one of these, aware that they were a unique and fast-disappearing anomaly within Anglicanism as a whole. I still found the *Novus Ordo* theologically unsatisfactory in parts, but less so than the more modernist formulations of *Common Worship*, which was then being introduced elsewhere.

My general unease with the changes that beset the Church of England at that time was linked to my increasing political awareness. I had been fortunate to grow up during an era where the core values of a civilized society were generally maintained across the political spectrum, notwithstanding differences of emphasis and methodology. During my later adolescence, the aggressive spread of postmodernism and the ideological takeover of most areas of cultural import by elements of the doctrinaire, atheist Left threatened ideas and moral precepts that I believed were essential for the continued upholding of the core message of freedom, individual conscience, and personal responsibility conveyed by the Gospels. This process intensified in the wake of the fall of the Soviet Union and the Eastern bloc, when the far Left poured their energies from direct political engagement into parapolitical social transformation.

These were the days when the evangelical and most particularly, fundamentalist elements were gaining significant ground in the Anglican communion. I found no experience of the mystery of God in their forms of worship, and indeed rejected many of the tawdry manifestations that masqueraded as "the gifts of the Spirit" almost from instinct, together with the selective Biblical literalism that was at their heart. I saw what they were doing as an attack—perhaps not intended as such, but nevertheless effective—upon the beauty, peace, and tradition that I saw as being at the heart of profound communion with the Divine, together with individual freedom of conscience, which was thrown aside in the new rush to dogmatism. Unfortunately, the Anglican theological colleges in the London area had almost entirely given themselves over to the evangelical approach, and that tendency was also becoming widespread beyond the capital. I could certainly see no place for myself within this new-style Anglican ministry, nor had I much in the way of common theological ground with the priests I met who had graduated from of these institutions.

I began to speak out at that time against the trend towards fundamentalism, intolerance, and the decline of traditional worship, and united this philosophically with my political stance of classical liberalism. When *The Times* produced a particularly mean-spirited obituary of Bishop Masters, my letter was one of those it published among what was said to have been a record number of complaints on such a matter. I perceived the changing directions in the Church and in academia to be common manifestations of the same doctrinaire socialist reinforcement of new, false orthodoxies, and my duty lie in opposing these falsehoods. Such a course of action would likely mean embracing isolation and rejection, but these were not conditions that any Christian should have genuine cause to fear.

The consequence of the stand that I took, and its inevitable questioning of the establishments concerned, was that it became effectively impossible for me to work within the mainstream academic and artistic spheres, where the Left held sway. Despite having graduated from the Royal College of Music with a dozen prizes as the top pianist of my year, I was effectively branded as a dissident there and at Cambridge, where I undertook some of my postgraduate education, and the patronage that was by then the only means of rising in those fields was firmly withheld.

These experiences served to strengthen my convictions towards classical liberalism, and since I had no difficulty in reconciling those beliefs with my liberal but traditionalist Christian faith, I resolved to seek an expression of that faith that would uphold what I believed to be its essence. Alongside this, I continued to work as a musician, writer, and teacher, seeking positions entirely within the private sector in order to achieve the ideological freedom that I perceived as essential. During this time I found my teaching to be an excellent outlet for ministry to young people who, despite often coming from wealthy backgrounds, were troubled and who needed guidance as they found their way in life. In retrospect, this experience was an excellent preparation for my future vocation.

I became aware of the independent sacramental movement through several sources. In the first place, my interest in the preservation of the histories of those colleges and universities that had worked outside the state system brought me into contact with those educational establishments that had been part of Independent Catholicism both in the context of the training of ordinands and more broadly in ambitious attempts to create "alternative universities". I undertook a master's degree by distance learning in these areas under the guidance of a former president of the pioneering Mercy College in New York, and perceived that in the successes and failures of these institutions was the expression of what remained an urgent need both practically and philosophically for choices in tertiary education that were independent of governmental and education-establishment control.

The second focus of my attention on the independent sacramental movement was through an increasing awareness that it could offer the opportunity I sought for a Christian life that I could come to terms with. I was deeply attracted to a movement that did not equate the Church with power, hierarchy, and property, and where the majority gave their vocations without seeking monetary reward, rather than as a "career move." As someone whose own background was firmly in the working-class, I was also much taken with the fact that, at least in England, the ISM had been and continued to be a grass-roots movement with none of the distinctions of class or educational background still apparent in the established churches.

Although I had enjoyed some aspects of my teaching career greatly, and had seen a number of my students achieve recognition at national level, the tendencies toward ideological uniformity and micro-management that had driven me from the state sector were now starting to infect the private further education colleges where I had been working. In particular, the renewed emphasis on conformity and submission to external oversight of various dubious kinds removed much of the vital creative spirit from the sector and filled me with a heavy heart. It was time to look for something new, and during my final years in teaching I sought to put something of a framework in place that might point the way for the future.

I had continued my private reading in theology, and in 2001 made first contact with the Rev. Dr. H.J. Zitko of Arizona, who had moved from full-time Christian ministry in the 1960s to the founder presidency of the World University, an international humanitarian organization. Dr. Zitko had immersed himself in the esoteric philosophies of Theosophy, the Rosicrucians, and the Arcane School of Alice Bailey. These were subjects I was keen to learn more of, and I completed his thirteen-month correspondence course that outlined each of these aspects in detail and melded them into a coherent philosophy. He and I corresponded on spiritual and practical matters, and in 2003 he was to write to me, "Again, thank you for everything. You are one of the most valued members in our world institution." That was to be our last contact before he passed to spirit the following year. When today I sign off a letter with the greeting "In Light and Life," it is in tribute to Dr. Zitko, for whom that was not only a habitual salutation, but the reality of his spiritual existence.

On completion of Dr. Zitko's course, I began discussion with several colleagues that would lead to the formation that year of the Religious Society of St. Katharine under the presidency of the assistant superior of the Josephite order in England. The RSStK was an ecumenical Christian community that was geographically widespread but united in liberal precept, and at its close had around fifteen members. The Society ran its own distance learning theological college, registered with the State of Wyoming, USA, and offered all courses free of charge, with myself and its other tutors working without payment.

In 2005, serious personal differences emerged among the directors of the Society as the outcome of external politics involving other institutions. Regrettably, these issues were to result in the Society's demise along with its college. The constitution had been drawn up in such a way that I could not carry on the work of the Society on my own initiative, despite no-one else wishing to do so, and was instead compelled to start afresh.

I had known Fr. Andrew Linley since around 1997, and at some point a few years later met his fellow minister the Rev. George Stephen Callander. Stephen was a gifted clergyman with an active funeral ministry and was personally a most engaging character. He had been priested within the Old Roman Catholic Church of Great Britain in

1993, a denomination that effectively came to an end when its Archbishop, Douglas Titus Lewins, reconciled with the Holy See in 1998. Searching for a freer approach to Catholicism, Stephen had in 1999 founded a small group first known as the British Liberal Free Church and its associated Society of Free Christians—inspired by the Rev. J.M. Lloyd Thomas and his Society of Free Catholics. This group was seeking to promote a liberal Catholicism within a Unitarian tradition that had long since disappeared from the mainstream of that denomination. Andrew had, like me, initially been ordained in another community, but had been incardinated as a minister into the SFC in 2003 and had taken on further responsibilities in due time.

The SFC worshipped in the side-chapel at Bloomsbury Baptist Church for some years, and also held services in the chapel of the YMCA at Wimbledon. As well as specially-composed liturgies that at times achieved considerable beauty, the Prayer Book of the King's Chapel, Boston, was in use. In time, I was incardinated into the denomination, which changed its name in 2005 to the English Liberal Free Church, and at the same time awarded the church's licentiateship diploma in theology for ministry. As well as being one of the three Ministers, I was also the church's Chancellor and took on responsibilities relating to its educational outreach, which was at that time active through several small correspondence colleges. Under my guidance, these colleges were consolidated into a single institution, Marquess College, which was directed under the auspices of the ELFC.

As 2006 dawned, ELFC was on a stable footing and in a strong position to look towards growth and outreach.

Some time ago, we had made an approach to the main body of Unitarians in England with a view to becoming accepted as a mainstream Unitarian congregation, but had been rejected for being "too Christian." This development served to deepen the Catholic awareness that distinguished our community from others, and to increase our feeling that the ISM was a setting within which we could enhance our ministry, chiefly through the blessing of Apostolic ordination. My reading of +John Plummer's works on the ISM in particular convinced me that a new and positive chapter was opening in its history, and that God was leading us towards the ISM as a means of developing our community. In my theological studies, this was also a time when the works of Matthew Fox, +John Mabry, Meister Eckhart and +Jonathan Blake began to have particular resonance for me, and my own position became closer to that of Process Theology. Since that time, I have additionally been led towards a deeper appreciation of Gnosticism, Theosophy, and the Eastern traditions, particularly elements of Buddhism and Hinduism.

In consequence of all this, and with all involved expressing views in favor, we began to have serious discussions about the practical steps necessary to receive the blessing of Apostolic ordination. Unfortunately there was no pre-extant ISM community in England that combined our vision of Catholic worship with a liberal, non-dogmatic context, with most communities instead being highly traditionalist and conservative in nature. There were further organisational and doctrinal issues that caused us at that time to put aside the possibility of an approach to the various churches of the Liberal Catholic movement in England, despite the fact that it was with

them that we had most in common. Our eventual conclusion was that it was not desirable at that time to join or
amalgamate with another church.

Consequently, what we needed to seek was a bishop
with a Catholic understanding of the nature of Holy
Orders who would be prepared to bestow those orders
specifically for our community, without requiring an oath
of canonical obedience, and to consecrate one of our
number to the episcopate as a means of establishing our
community as an independent, autocephalous entity.

Our search was not an easy one, because the number of
bishops that would be prepared to consider such a pro-
posal was necessarily small, and because there were many
bishops whom we considered unsuitable for a number of
reasons. However, our contact with Archbishop Illtyd
Thomas, Primate of the Celtic Catholic Church, was a
positive one, and he expressed a willingness to assist us.
In keeping with the equal nature and position of our three
ministers, it was proposed and agreed at that time that
Andrew and I should receive the episcopate, and then that
the two of us should consecrate Stephen in turn.
Archbishop Thomas, who had been consecrated by
Archbishops Walter Williams, Primate of the Holy Celtic
Church, and Bertil Persson, Primate of the Apostolic
Episcopal Church, united in his person all the major lines
of Apostolic Succession. He was 88 years old when we
met him, and although suffering periodic ill-health, was
still mentally acute, vigorous in speech, and pugnacious
in demeanor.

Some aspects of Archbishop Thomas' life and work
have been rightly regarded as difficult and controversial,
and contribute to the complexity of making any just

assessment of his achievement. Rather than dwell on those aspects, I should say that I will remain grateful for his very considerable generosity towards our church and for the personal warmth and hospitality, underpinned by deep and unquestioning faith, that he showed towards Andrew and myself during the period of our ordination and consecration. Believing that ours would be his final consecration after twenty-eight years as a bishop, he donated all his official papers as well as many books to us, which have formed an invaluable archive. Having been admitted as a bishop of the Liberal Catholic Church of Ontario in 1986, he was happy to consecrate us in that tradition, using the 1967 edition of +Wedgwood's beautiful liturgy. In accordance with our agreement, we did not execute instruments of canonical obedience or become members of Archbishop Thomas' church, and the context of the services and attesting documentation was that of the wider Old Catholic Church of the Ütrecht Succession rather than of his own denomination.

Consecration was inevitably a major event in my life, albeit one over which I had initially hesitated, before the experience of a vision established that it was indeed God's will for me. The event of consecration marked a significant stage in the path leading me towards future enlightenment, by which term I express the idea of an unbroken union with God, and, as further proof, I found my spiritual energies and attunement had increased considerably in the wake of that event. Yet this was only the start of many plans for our church and for my future life. I threw myself into an active funeral ministry, and used the Archbishop Thomas archive together with other documents now coming into our possession to undertake historical studies into the movement and to disseminate the knowledge that resulted as widely as possible using the internet. Archbishop Bertil Persson, my consecrator's consecrator, sent me warm good wishes and copies of several of his publications. ELFC began a weekly community Mass in Bishop Andrew's private oratory to which all were welcomed, using the Rite of the Liberal Catholic Church International.

It came as a complete surprise to Andrew and myself when, a month after our consecration, Stephen withdrew from his planned consecration and resigned altogether from his ministry in ELFC in order to enter a purely Unitarian practice. He had not enjoyed good health for some time, and was seeking to make major changes to his life. We were extremely sorry to bid him farewell, since his energy, good humor, and spiritual gifts had been a driving force in helping to make ELFC what it was, yet equally we recognised that his path through faith could not be constrained.

This time of change set in place a transitional period for ELFC. Using the temporary name of the Independent Old Catholic Church of the Ütrecht Succession (IOCCUS), we undertook a re-organisation so that all elements of our small membership would continue to be served while necessarily accommodating both the changed context of our church and the changes in clergy that had taken place. During this period, we were contacted by the traditionalist Archbishop Phillip Kemp of the Independent Catholic Alliance, and as a result agreed to undertake a service of mutual subconditional ordination and consecration according to the rite of the Roman Catholic Church in November 2006. This action brought new lines of

Apostolic Succession to both of our churches, and afforded us the additional blessing of ordination and consecration within the traditionalist Roman context to add to our earlier Liberal Catholic Holy Orders.

By January 2007, the transition was complete, and we took on our new name of The Liberal Rite, with the other divisions of ELFC now reconstituted as the Religious Society of St. Simon and the Society for Humanistic Potential. Later in the year, we would expand the distance learning educational outreach of the former Marquess College through the launch of the new European-American University (with its specialist Arnold Harris Mathew Center for the Study of the Independent Sacramental Movement).

During that month, working with Msgr. Alistair Bate (then of the Liberal Catholic Church International), we planned and launched the Independent Liberal Catholic Fellowship (ILCF) as an interdenominational fellowship for both "Liberal Catholics" and "liberal catholics" who were in Apostolic orders. This fellowship grew steadily through its first twelve months, embracing around twenty clergy from all around the world, a number of established communities, and one religious order (the Companions of the Cross and Passion).

An effort towards healing the divisions in the ISM, the ILCF offers an opportunity for those of liberal principle to come together in a co-operative, non-dogmatic, non-hierarchical setting where all are free to pursue their own spiritual path. I administered the ILCF since its outset, and dealt with its regular enquiries from international communities and clergy with other bishops. The ILCF now means that our mission encompasses chapels and oratories in both England and Scotland, including the beautiful Well Chapel in Suffolk. Working with Bishop Markus van Alphen in Holland, I and a number of other bishops in the ILCF became members of the Sophia Circle, an organisation of free bishops in the esoteric tradition associated with The Young Rite, which is a community member of the ILCF.

The Liberal Rite and the ILCF quickly became the focus of a steady stream of enquiries from individuals wishing to know more about Liberal Catholicism, as well as a number who were seeking ordination. We admitted our first postulants to formal candidacy for Holy Orders and currently support two candidates who are still completing their studies in preparation for ordination and a third who was ordained in January 2008. These numbers suggest at once that we are reaching those to whom we can be of help and that our policy of being selective and cautious in those who are accepted for ordination is paying off. Ordinands complete studies to the level of a Licentiateship and are also attached to a chapel or oratory in order to participate in the regular celebration of Mass and receive the necessary altar training.

It was a particular pleasure in August, 2007 for me to consecrate our first two bishops within the ILCF, Fr. Alistair Bate (formerly of the LCCI) and Fr. Charles Mugleston (formerly of the LCC) at the Well Chapel. Both are men of great qualities who have the capacity to lead others to an experience of the beauty of the love of God, and they have become mainstays of the ILCF as it has developed.

At the outset of the following year, a further key development was to occur. Some time previously, Richard

Hadingham, the senior surviving member of the Ancient Catholic Church based in London, had been moved to make contact with me. Richard had said to me that our contact had come about for a specific reason, and in January 2008 that purpose was to be revealed through a series of events that led to my commission to continue the work and ministry of the founder of the Ancient Catholic Church, Mar Joannes I (Archbishop Harold Nicholson). It was resolved that the +Nicholson legacy should be united with that of The Liberal Rite, and accordingly the Liberal Catholic Apostolic Church came into being as a fulfilment of the unity of these paths.

This action was dramatic in its results. Our church saw dynamic growth as new clergy joined us with their communities and people began to enquire about becoming seminarians. This brought into the church a number of people of proven spirituality and considerable accomplishment whose energies were then added to our existing strengths. We expanded to include a number of parishes in the United States as well as the United Kingdom and took the legal and other steps necessary to establish our church as a permanent and ongoing spiritual witness and to ensure that it had the capacity to fulfil its mission. As part of this, all the religious Orders and Societies that were previously part of our constituent churches now found themselves continued or revived as part of the new church.

The new church was firmly committed to ecumenism, standing at the meeting point of many different spiritual traditions through our largely Pre-Nicene stance, and our ongoing contact with Archbishop Bertil Persson deepened this mission which has been so considerable a part of his life's ministry. In mid-2008, acting on commission from Archbishop Francis Spataro, Primate of the Apostolic Episcopal Church, Archbishop Persson appointed me Archbishop-Elect of the Apostolic Episcopal Church for the UK, in succession to the late Bishop George Boyer. I was enthroned to that senior office by Archbishop Persson in November 2008, and in January 2009, as part of a general re-structuring of responsibilities, retired from my positions in the Liberal Catholic Apostolic Church, while remaining in communion with and continuing to advise that church.

No account of this history would be complete without mentioning the steadfast example and vision of my colleague and brother bishop Andrew Linley, whose support has been essential both to our achievements and to the friendly and co-operative spirit in which they have been realised. The Liberal Catholic Apostolic Church owes him so much.

This essentially takes us up to the present day and the latest chapter in this story. As I write, I realise the tremendous fulfilment that I have gained from my involvement with the ISM. Currently, in addition to the responsibilities of regular worship and the administration of the church and the ILCF worldwide, I take around fifty funerals each year, direct European-American University and its Mathew Center (undertaking research into the ISM and promulgating source material relating to it both online and in books), make recordings and give occasional concerts as a pianist, and continue to provide consultancy on educational matters aimed at securing social justice for those unfairly facing discrimination and disadvantage.

Today, I realise how much I look towards nature and

the imaginative life that stems from it for my continued experience of the presence of God. I am fortunate to live on the borders of the countryside, and my garden is filled with wild birds which are a particular pleasure. I believe that we should not only speak to God, but also listen to what He wants to say to us, and I try to leave room in a busy existence to do just that. Art, literature, music, nature; these are all ways in which the transcendence that first drew me to the Divine continues to manifest itself and to convey His blessings.

This is the life I would choose given a free choice; it is the life to which I thank God for leading me. It remains only to trust in Him and look to His guiding wisdom for the future.

The Most Rev. Ronald Langham,
DD, BDiv, JP

Archbishop, United Ecumenical
Catholic Church—Australia

# "With Windows Open to the Holy Spirit"

TRYING TO RESPOND TO Bishop Bate's request for a
"mini-bio" was perhaps one of the harder things I have
attempted in many years. In some ways my spiritual journey is unique, as are all of our journeys. Yet I have no
doubt that many of us will also hold common experiences, motivators, etc. None the less, I offer my own small
contribution for what it is worth.

My first experience of "vocation" was as a ten-year-old.
A product of the good (and some not so good) Sisters of
St. Joseph of the Sacred Heart, and that confusing time
immediately following Vatican II, perhaps I was destined
to at least consider a life as a priest or religious. From that
age until around fifteen, I wanted nothing more than to be
a Sacred Heart Missionary (MSC). I wanted to emulate my
boyhood hero, St. Dominic Savio, and be perfect, as I considered him to be. Like many good Roman Catholic boys
of the times, I was an Altar-boy, and lived my life in awe

of priests, nuns, and religious. I tried my very best to be worthy of sainthood, although I was in no rush to achieve it in the ordinary sense.

My years between ages ten and fifteen were uneventful; the usual high school stuff where, whenever I was asked, I was quick to sate that I was going to be a priest. Given that we were well and truly entrenched in post-Vatican II thought, and the desire to be a saint was no longer a popular choice amongst Catholic schoolboys, I was viewed as somewhat of an oddity by so many of my school friends.

My conviction, though, continued and at the age of seventeen I joined a fairly new (fifteen years young), Australian religious order of brothers. The main apostolate of the order was to give religious education to young Catholic students who attended State (Government) schools and did not have the ongoing blessing of the presence of Brothers or Sisters who were so quick to point out any flaw of character in those of us who were so blessed with their presence.

The order I joined was young both in establishment years and in the chronological age of most of the Brothers. The Founder, also our Superior General, was only thirty-six years old at the time I joined. My novice Master was only twenty-six, and so many of the postulants and novices were sixteen or seventeen, like me. Sadly, my journey with the good brothers was not to last and, in just under twelve months, I decided that I was not yet ready for a life-time commitment such as this. The reasons for leaving were mine alone and in no way reflected upon the Order.

The next six years were somewhat of a blur and a spiritual desert. I worked in various industries including cooking in mining camps and on a cattle ranch until I finally joined the Australian Public Service, in which I remained for the next ten years. I call this intervening period a "spiritual desert" because it was during this time that I came to realise that I was gay and this just did not sit well with my well-formed Roman Catholic values and understandings.

I was basically in a conundrum. Here I was, a good Catholic boy, still single at 22, sexually inactive and basically hiding myself in work. Around this time I met a woman who was to become my wife, the mother of my children, and the bane of my life. The marriage was to last ten years and dissolved, not because of sexuality issues, but simply because we were destroying each other emotionally and spiritually.

At age thirty-six I finally came out of the closet and embraced my sexual identity. I was ready to walk away from a church that did not want me because of my sexuality but I still felt a call to ministry. How could this be? I did receive a "Freedom to Marry" from my local Roman Bishop which meant that I could also be ordained if such were ever a consideration, however Roman teaching meant that I could not be both honest with them as well as be a priest with them. My true journey began.

In the late 1990s while visiting a friend in jail (a former RC priest), I met with a former brother from the religious order to which I had previously belonged, and he mentioned a thing called "autocephalous bishops". I had never heard of such a thing and he went on to explain, as best he could, who and what they were. Thank God for the internet! I spent the following months learning everything I could about this wonderful world of Old and

Independent Catholicism. I became somewhat of an expert on the various churches out there, the Apostolic Succession, etc. I found an independent Bishop in another Australian State and, after a period of chatting, exploring etc, he ordained me as a priest. I was never to be a member of his church though, as quite frankly, their beliefs were somewhat too esoteric for me. Nonetheless, his orders were valid according to Roman teaching and that was all I cared about at the time.

My mission, as I chose to accept it (☺), was to reach out to the disenfranchised Catholics of Sydney, Australia's largest city. I wanted to be able to offer the sacraments to those who were denied them by Rome; gays, lesbians, the divorced, anyone who felt they were not welcome at the altar of their local Roman Catholic church. The days of my unequivocal adherence to the rules of Rome were gone. I discovered people like John Shelby Spong, a great thinker who made me think about all the religious tripe that I had been force-fed for the past 40+ years.

After some period of time, I found myself isolated and "alone," even with my newfound mission. I sensed a need to be part of something larger; I needed to belong to a "real church." Again, the internet came to my rescue. After several inquiries, I approached one particular church in the USA with a view to joining them. I was astonished to be both accepted and asked if I would become their Bishop for Australia. I accepted with a sense of trepidation and humility. I barely had a congregation, how could I also be a bishop? Little was I to know that any form of congregation was more than many bishops had.

I was consecrated Bishop on February 3rd, 2001. Not unlike most of the other bishops in the same jurisdiction my relationship with my jurisdiction did not last. This was the first lesson on a rather large learning curve; I discovered that a large number of people within the OC/IC movement were really no more than pale imitations of Rome, with the same sense of "Papal" control; sadly this desire for control (by the "Patriarch") did not come to the surface until after my consecration. In less than twelve months I had left that jurisdiction to form our own church in Australia.

Within the first three years of my episcopacy I had ordained a number of priests, mainly people with a background in religious life or with some seminary training. My old novice master became my greatest advisor and my personal chaplain. Despite the enthusiasm of so many— clergy, friends, family, etc., we did not achieve any great numbers in the pews, something that continues to this day. This is, I think, a symptom of the spiritual ill-health of the western world rather than an indicator of the state of the OC movement.

In many ways, though, our small church achieved more than most OC/IC churches. Within two years we had missions in three States of Australia and had established a welfare service for homeless people, providing over 6,000 bed nights per year to homeless men and women, and over 16,000 meals per year to these same clients. We now have two services for homeless people, provide over 16,000 bed nights per year, almost 50,000 meals per year, and we employ 12 staff on a full-time basis. We also have a retail store that services the devotional needs of Christians; this is a fairly new venture but one that allows us to reach out to the general population and also helps to finance our welfare works.

Within three years of being made a Bishop I was able to leave secular employment and work full-time in ministry, and still maintain a reasonable level of income and lifestyle. This is basically unheard of in the OC/IC movement. Our achievements did not mean we were "better" than others; perhaps it just meant we were a little more organised than others. The reasons are for others to judge. It remains that we have done what so many others have not been able.

For all of our achievements there remained a sense of isolation. Despite my priests, deacons, charitable work etc., I felt that we were isolated from the rest of the OC movement and had not fulfilled the requirements of the Priestly Prayer of Jesus. I went searching once again.

In my search God has blessed me greatly with the friendship and support of Archbishop Terry Flynn of the United Kingdom. Together with +Terry I sought to bring together a number of smaller churches with a similar ecclesiology and theology in the knowledge that true strength lay in unity, true unity—not the "feel-good unity" of intercommunion agreements which basically amounted to nothing more than the paper they were written on. As is so often the case, the theory is one thing, the experience another. After much work and many promises, three small jurisdictions came together to form the United Ecumenical Catholic Church. It started with such great promise; it ended as a result of ego, the downfall of so many OC/IC jurisdictions. It does no one any good to dwell on the people, the perjury, or the perdition; I am sure many will understand when I simply say that "it hurt" that so much faith had lead to so little. We were not the first to fail, nor I fear, will we be the last.

The United Ecumenical Catholic Church, though, lives on, and remains committed to its original goals of being an open, accepting, and affirming church in the "small c" catholic tradition. It remains committed to being an "accountable" church, devoid of the hierarchy or pomposity of other churches. It remains committed to being a church that is identifiable in its own right and is not mistaken for Rome or Canterbury. At the same time we remain committed to the Priestly Prayer of Jesus that we "may all be one." We leave open the door of union and acceptance to Rome and all others who have cut themselves off from the church universal. The windows of the UECC are open always to the workings of the Holy Spirit. I give thanks for those Bishops who share my vision— especially Archbishop Terry Flynn and Bishop Jack Isbell—friends and spiritual co-travellers.

My spiritual journey continues and will do so until I meet with my maker. My time in the OC/IC movement has been one of great spiritual growth; I have learned the difference between faith and religion. I have learned the difference between church and community. I have learned the difference between ministry and delusions of religious grandeur. I have learned that being "non-Canonical" does not mean having lesser standards or expectations than the larger churches.

I give thanks for the OC/IC movement; it has the potential to be a spiritual force for the good of the people of God. It has the potential to be truly prophetic but it needs, like all churches, renewal. The O/IC movement needs to be a place of nourishment and safety for the people of God, rather than a refuge for delusional self-made Patriarchs and alternative Popes. For this to happen it needs leaders who are prepared to be unpopular; leaders who are prepared to be like Christ and throw the dealers out of the temple; leaders who are more concerned with accountability and true ministry rather than the titles and the false idols of pomp and pomposity. I look forward to being on ongoing part of that movement.

The Rt. Rev. John R. Mabry, PhD

Old Catholic Order
of Holy Wisdom

# "Wrestling with God"

THE BIBLICAL STORY THAT BEST represents my spiritual journey is that of Jacob wrestling with the angel (Gen 32:24-32). After the match—which takes all night—Jacob emerges with both a limp and a blessing. He also gets a new name, "Israel," which, in Hebrew, means "one who wrestles with God." I keep a decoupage icon of Doré's woodcut of that scene nearby when I need to be reminded that I'm not alone in this dangerous enterprise. We are all called to wrestle with God. So what if I have taken it to Olympic proportions?

My wrestling began as a boy raised in a moderate Southern Baptist family. Born near Los Angeles, we moved to the Midwest when I was six. My father was a federal agent and was moved around a lot, so we rarely stayed in one place for long. But whenever we finished unpacking the house, the first order of business was to find a Southern Baptist church.

I was generally happy in my family's religious life, and the churches we belonged to were wonderful communities of faith that I remember with fondness. They gave me many gifts—an appreciation of the value of spiritual community, and a biblical literacy that would serve me well later in life.

That all changed when, in High School, my family joined a church in Illinois that was influenced by the arch-fundamentalist theology of Jack Hyles and Bob Jones. It was nominally a Southern Baptist Church, but theologically it was very much in the Independent Baptist camp. My parents were not too sure at first, but the youth group was so vibrant, so exciting and inviting, that my sister and I prevailed and we became members. It was to be one of the biggest mistakes of our lives.

The leadership of this church was autocratic and secretive, and it's methods abusive. We youth were terrorized with sermons about the hellfire that certainly awaited all of those who did not embrace our peculiar theology. We were drilled in "witnessing" techniques and threatened that God would hold us accountable for every person we encountered that we did not witness to, that their blood would be upon our hands at the Judgment.

I experienced a horrendous psychodrama in which our youth group was confronted by men in strange uniforms wielding machine guns informing us that the United States had been taken over by an atheistic power, and that all Christians who would not renounce Christ would be summarily executed. And then we watched as our own youth pastor was dragged, kicking and screaming to the moonlit lawn below. He was given a chance to renounce his savior, and he shook his head in defiance. One of the occupying soldiers then shot him in the back of the head and we all watched in horror as his body pitched forward and the "crack" of the pistol reverberated through the woods. We weren't told it wasn't real until we arrived home, white-faced and shitting ourselves.

It is a much longer story, and there were many other examples of the spiritual abuse that was rampant in that place, but that will suffice as an illustration for our purposes here. Unfortunately I bought into the whole package, and even surrendered to preach. I believe I may have been the youngest person licensed to preach in the Southern Baptist Convention, and at sixteen years old I found myself on top of a table at the nearby rollar rink waving my big red Bible and telling everyone they were going to Hell.

Eventually, and providentially, my father put in for a transfer back to California, in part, I believe, to remove us from that church.

We found another church, but by that time it was too late. I was so traumatized by our experience that I rejected Christianity altogether, and when my friends got into sex, drugs, and rock-n-roll, I was in for the ride. But between my burgeoning sexual appetite and acid experiences, my spiritual hunger did not abate. I read voraciously on various world religions, especially Sufism and Buddhism. I also began a life-long love affair with Jewish and Christian apocryphal and pseudipigraphal literature.

But no amount of intellectual curiosity could fill the aching void I felt in my soul. Finally, blind drunk in my girlfriend's parking lot at four in the morning, I cried out to the heavens, "I cannot believe in the God of my parents, but if there's anybody out there, please please please let me know!"

Twenty-four hours later my girlfriend and I were in the back seat of my best friend Bob's car. We, along with Bob and his girlfriend, were headed to Disneyland. Sometime during that journey I asked Bob what God was. He thought for a moment, and then began to describe the universe as a vast, seemingly chaotic, but ultimately highly-ordered dance. Everything in creation knew the steps to the dance—the angels, the demons, the planets, the stars, the oceans, the plants and animals. Everything stepped joyfully and in time. All except for humans—we had forgotten the steps to the dance, and our religious traditions are but feeble attempts to remember the steps.

This image hit me with the force of a revelation and I cried for three days. Simple as the image was, I knew in my heart that it was, for me, true. From that moment on, I was a universalist. It is still an image that has great meaning for me. And as much as I believe anything, I believe *that*.

So what to do with my newfound religious understanding? Because my culture—and my own heritage—was Christian, it made sense to dance that dance, understanding it contained only a partial degree of truth. It was my history, my inheritance, and I set out to be the best "Christian"—as I now understood the term—as I could. I joined a Baptist church that specialized in worship through the arts, and began writing and performing Christian rock music with a fervor. I also got my ear pierced as a covenant between myself and God—a kind of idiosyncratic circumcision—so that every time I looked in the mirror I would remember who I really was, and would never again fall back into the trap of fundamentalist conformity.

This was a form of Christianity my girlfriend could stomach, so she was baptized, and we married soon after. A month later we headed down to Riverside, California, so I could begin to attend California Baptist College. It was a precious and transformative time. I met there people who would deeply impact me, and many who are still close friends and colleagues in ministry. But the person I met there that impacted me the most was Jesus.

It started in an English literature class. We were reading Robert Browning's poem, "Caliban Upon Setebos," which is based on Shakespeare's *The Tempest*. Caliban is the monster than inhabits the island on which the play is set, and Setebos is what he names his god. Because Caliban is cruel and capricious, he projects his own nature onto his god, and grovels before him, begging for the mercy that he refuses to show to others. At the time I read that poem I had been suffering from terrifying nightmares of hellfire from which I awoke screaming and sweating—no doubt a product of the fundamentalist environment in which I found myself. The poem forced me to confront the fact that the god I had been given as a child was a monster and not worthy of my devotion. It is, I realized, impossible to love a monster. I came to understand that faith born of fear is not true faith at all, but extortion.

As I was wrestling with this epiphany, a friend of mine said, "Hey, let's go see what C.S. Lewis and Charles Williams meant by 'church.'" We were both huge Lewis and Williams fans, and the idea intrigued me, so the next Sunday morning found us at St. Michael's Episcopal Church.

I was awed by the beauty of the sanctuary. Unlike Baptist churches, which eschew beauty or ornamentation,

St. Michael's was a feast for the senses. My eyes were assaulted by beauty everywhere I looked, the organ and choral music was nothing short of glorious, and the incense sent me into an altered state. And the enormous, gory crucifix hanging over the center of the room revealed, in no uncertain terms, the lengths God was willing to go to in order to express his love for me. I was utterly overwhelmed and when communion was announced, I raced to the rail.

As I knelt and the priest laid the host on my tongue, I felt a Presence wash over me and an audible voice whispered in my ear, "This is my mercy for you—feel it, taste it. It's *real*." I wept as I returned to my seat. There, in the sanctity of this little Anglican community, I had, for the first time in my life, actually encountered the living Christ.

I dragged my wife to the Episcopal church, which she preferred to the Bible-thumping of the Baptists, and within a year we were both confirmed. I continued to struggle with the theology of Paul, and when I complained to my priest, Fr. Gene looked at me with compassion and said simply, "Your relationship isn't with Paul. Ignore Paul. Follow Jesus."

More liberating words were never spoken, and I gloried in the fact that the whole of the Christian tradition was now mine. Baptist history leads you to believe that there was a seventeen-hundred-year gap of apostasy between the primitive Christian church and the founding of the first Baptist congregation in Rhode Island. But now, I came to realize, I had an heritage for the first time. Anglicanism is a form of Catholicism, after all, and I reclaimed the whole of the Orthodox, Catholic, and

Protestant history as my own. For the first time I felt I had *roots*, and a deep connection to those saints who had gone before me.

I continued as an ardent Anglican as I finished my studies and moved north to begin a Master's Degree in Creation Spirituality at Matthew Fox's Institute at Holy Names College in Oakland. There I nervously studied witchcraft with Starhawk, discovered the Perennial Philosophy, and recognized the deep mysticism shared by all spiritual traditions, even as I plumbed the depths of my own. I connected again with Bob's vision of the dancing universe with renewed and profound appreciation.

It was during my studies that friends began asking me to do life-cycle rituals for them, in the Wiccan tradition. Now, I was not a witch, but I had learned enough of the basics in Starhawk's class to satisfy the needs of my friends, and the experience reawakened in me the call that had caused me to surrender to preach all those years ago. I discerned that God was calling me to be a priest, and set about figuring out how that might happen.

Investigating the Episcopal Seminary, I was told that three years of study there would cost me $35,000. I felt crushed. I was already $20,000 in debt from my undergraduate studies, and could not take on much more. And, certainly, $35,000 felt like too much. Besides, I came from a tradition where most people were poor—since Baptists want well-educated clergy, seminarians don't pay a dime. Historically, though, Episcopalians are rich, and their seminarians pay their own way. I was an oxymoron—a poor Episcopalian, and I saw no way ahead. I wrestled greatly with this call and finally, I prayed, "God, I believe you want me to follow you into the priesthood, but I seem to have hit a brick wall. What do you want me to do?"

Again, my desperate prayer was answered promptly. Within a week, I met the acquaintance of a bishop of the Old Catholic succession. He accepted my master's degree in spirituality, mentored me in some private study, and ordained me—first to the diaconate, and then a few months later, to the priesthood. I couldn't have been happier. God had found a way.

For the first few years, my ministry consisted of chaplaincy work in nearby convalescent hospitals—my work in an Alzheimer's unit was especially meaningful. But God had other plans for me.

While studying at Holy Names, I was hired as an editorial assistant for *Creation Spirituality* magazine. Eventually I was promoted to managing editor, and, finally editor, of that fine publication. My wife and I divorced during that time—an amicable parting of ways—and I moved into an apartment near the magazine offices, rooming with a friend from Cal Baptist. I began looking for a spiritual community, and opening the Yellow Pages, discovered an ad for what sounded like a very odd place in North Berkeley—the Grace Institute for Religious Learning.

When I stepped into their historic, arts-and-crafts style sanctuary, I was floored by the surreal sight of a Roman Forum. Berkeley Opera, apparently, was renting the sanctuary on Saturday nights for their performances, and so Mass was being said in the Temple of Athena. I smiled at the oddness all the way through the service, conducted by a British priest who reminded me very much of Alan Watts, both in terms of looks and impishness.

I hung around after the service to talk to him, and he

said, "Could you just grab the vessels, there, and help me bring them into the sacristy?"

"Of course," I replied. "I *am* a priest after all."

"Really?" His eyes lit up and after coffee hour we spent at least ninety minutes getting to know each other. From that moment forward, I assisted Fr. Richard at the altar, and was soon called to be their associate pastor.

Not long after, I married again—to a fellow recovering fundamentalist I had met in a Fundamentalists Anonymous group I had been running. Kate didn't like the conservative Anglican liturgy of the church I had found, and the congregation didn't like her opinionated brashness. So I went to church alone, and as of this writing, am still serving there, as pastor.

Meanwhile, I continued my studies, earning a PhD in World Religions from the California Institute of Integral Studies (a bargain at $15,000 at the time), and continued my editorial tent-making as editor of *Presence*, the worldwide professional journal for spiritual directors. During this time I also suffered a second divorce, and underwent several painful personal crises as I continued to wrestle with the path God set before me.

Grace North Church, however, became a great source of grace, and my true vocation. It is an odd parish, with a disproportionate number of British ex-pats, virtually guaranteeing a high eccentricity quotient. The church went through many vicissitudes and changes, but essentially it has always been Anglican in liturgy, Congregational in polity (and denominational affiliation), and nearly Unitarian in teaching and theology.

Most striking, however, was how it understood its Congregational polity. Fr. Richard had brilliantly re-cast the traditional categories of virginity, chastity, and celibacy into the political (rather than sexual) arena. Therefore the clergy at our church are celibate—not sexually celibate, but *politically* celibate. This means we have no administrative duties or responsibilities whatsoever. We make no decisions and tell no one what to do. We preach, teach, and visit the sick, and absolutely nothing else. The people run the church by consensus, which liberates the clergy to actually do our jobs as ministers.

It is also our job to protect the *virginity* of all of our parishioners—to remind them that they own their own power and should not give it away to anyone. Likewise, we remind parishioners to be *chaste* in their exercise of power—to share it equally and not to bully one another or usurp another's power. All parishioners have one vote at our quarterly meeting, where all the large decisions are made. The only people who do not have a vote—which includes children under thirteen, canine parishioners, and the clergy—still have voice, and must be offered an opportunity to be heard before a vote commences.

The wonderful thing about this system is that it almost eliminates the abuse of power that I have seen, time and again, destroy other spiritual communities. And it works very, very well. If, as Paul says, Jesus emptied himself of power and took the form of a servant (Phil. 2:7), then those of us who serve in his name should do likewise.

It is this very philosophy that has led to my consecration to the episcopacy, in fact. For years I watched my friends in the ministry—especially my female friends—getting jerked around by what I affectionately like to call "asshole bishops." There are a lot of asshole bishops out there, in the Independent Catholic movement as well as the larger Communions, and I'm sure everyone reading this knows at least one story of such a prelate.

In any case, I was getting fed up with the treatment of my friends, and an idea began to form. What if we created a jurisdiction—perhaps a religious order—that was entirely egalitarian? What if all vowed members—whether lay, deacons, priests, or bishops—all held equal power in the community? What if all decisions were made by consensus, and all members—at whatever order of ministry—had one vote? The more I thought and prayed about it the more I was certain that such a body could be successful in being a just container for our Catholicism.

In order for us to be a valid, autocephalous jurisdiction, however, we would need a bishop. I took the idea to Carol Vaccariello, an Independent Catholic bishop who was also an administrator at Matthew Fox's Creation Spirituality University. As we sat on the lawn overlooking Oakland's Lake Merrit, she smiled and said, "John, I *love* the idea. I will gladly share equal power with you and with the order members."

Within a few weeks I had put out a call, and nearly ten people showed up for the first meeting. Working as a consensus body, we talked through every issue required in constructing our rule. It took a lot of talk, but it was worth it, and we became a real community in the process. We took St. Sophia as our patron, and in 2006, the first members of the Old Catholic Order of Holy Wisdom covenanted together as a community and a jurisdiction.

Our first covenanting service was both joyful, and sad, because it was at that meeting that our beloved Bishop Carol announced that she and her husband would be moving to Ohio. She nominated me as her successor, a suggestion that the order members unanimously approved after an appropriate period of discernment. On April 22, 2007, Bishop Carol consecrated me for service to the Order, assisted by Bishops Rusty Clyma, Rob Angus Jones, and Rosamonde Miller.

I see now that a part of my mission and calling is to teach and model an ecclesiology that is truly based on the example of Jesus—of service and the joyful eschewing of all power-over—an alternative to the abusive tradition of hierarchy that has for millennia plagued the Christian community.

In addition to my service to my parish and the order, my ministry is rich in many other ways. I have published widely on spiritual guidance, world religions, and spirituality, and I am privileged to teach these subjects at such marvelous institutions as John F. Kennedy University, the Institute of Transpersonal Psychology, the University of Phoenix, and the Chaplaincy Institute for Arts and Interfaith Ministry.

Of course, I still continue to wrestle, but I see the blessing more and more in the struggle, and, well, I'm used to the limp by now. I like to think of myself as a Religious Agnostic, because I revel in the benefits of my spiritual communities and tradition, yet am committed to a non-dogmatic approach to the life of the spirit in which I acknowledge that what I think I know about God is minuscule in comparison to all that I do not know. But if pinned to the wall, I will admit that my cosmology is Whiteheadian; my theology, Unitarian; my Christology, Arian; and my soteriology, Abelardian and universalist. But my worship tradition is Catholic, specifically, Anglo-Catholic.

Along the way, I have met, prayed with, and struggled with many brilliant and sometimes troubled souls that I have been privileged to share this journey with, including (in alphabetical order) +Tim Barker, Lawson Barnes, +Lou Bordisso, Lucy Collier, Margaret Dana, Flavio Epstein, Lisa Fullam, +Charles Grande, Gina Rose Halpern, Sean Lynn, Cherrisa Mabry, Richard Mapplebeckpalmer+, Sean McConnell, Diane Miles+, Joan Morton, +John Plummer, Romeo Quintana, Jr., Ric Reed, Dennis Rivers, +River Sims, Donna Stoneham, Jan Thomas, Dan Turner+, +Carol Vaccariello, Richard Stevens+, B.J. West, Karyn Wolfe, all of the members, past and present, of the Old Catholic Order of Holy Wisdom, and many, many others too numerous to mention, but precious to me, all.

In the Independent Catholic movement I have found a home in which I enjoy the freedom to live authentically into the spiritual being God has made me to be, and still be firmly grounded in the whole history of our Christian heritage, the orthodox, saints and sinners, the heretics, mystics and misfits. They are all my family, united in following Jesus in our own idiosyncratic ways, all devoted to faithfully wrestling with an unfathomable God.

## The Old Catholic Order
## of Holy Wisdom Covenant               *Revised 2/24/06*

*I covenant with you, my brothers and sisters,*
*to seek after wisdom all my days,*
*for it is in searching after her that we find God;*
*and in searching after God that we find her.*
*It is through her counsel*
*that we build communities of compassion*
*and find refuge for our souls.*
*I will esteem her instruction more than silver*
*and her knowledge more than gold*               *Prov. 8:10*
*nor will I trust in riches,*
*but will find my treasure in her.*               *Prov. 2:1, 4*
*I promise to proclaim her wherever she may find me:*
*in the countryside, the villages,*
*and the busy tumult of the city.*
*To heed God is to be the mouthpiece of Wisdom,*
*to preach righteousness, justice,*
*and love for all creatures.*               *Prov. 2:8*
*Therefore I vow humility in all my affairs,*
*forsaking arrogance, neglect*               *Prov. 8:13*
*the unchaste use of people and creation,*
*and the exercise of power over others.*
*I promise to invite all peoples to Wisdom's banquet,*
*to offer her bread to the outcast and insider alike,*
*to give her wine to both the foolish and the wise,*               *Prov. 9:5*
*that all creation may taste of her goodness;*
*for the knowledge of her is sweeter than honey,*               *Sir. 24:20*
*all her ways are sacred,*
*and her paths all lead to peace.*               *Prov. 3:17*
*And I vow that I will not labor for myself alone,*
*but for all who truly seek Wisdom.*               *Sir. 24:30-34*

# The Most Rev. Rosamonde Miller

## Ecclesia Gnostica Mysteriorum

# "Wild Gnosis"

JUST AS WITH MANY OTHER things in my life, I didn't decide to become involved with the Independent Movement. It could arguably be said that I fell into it, but I would have answered yes to whatever field of action I was called to by this invisible, all-encompassing, and consuming power, which has more substance to me than this computer keyboard. But I'm getting ahead of myself. I should backtrack some eleven years prior to my initial connection with Independent Orders.

## Orly Airport, 14 kilometers South of Paris, January, 1962

I begin my story in the middle, for not all stories have a beginning. Often these beginnings are something that we invent in retrospect as linear markers to satisfy the mind's desire for concrete explanations; however, events just flow one into another to create a tapestry woven with interconnecting threads hued from the somber—even dismal—to the most riotously sunny. This middle of the story is not of my encounter with the Independent Catholic Movement, but one that, in my view, flows into it.

Tired and still sleepy after disembarking from the flight from Madrid, I crossed the tarmac toward the terminal in search of my pre-arranged ride into Paris. No one was there yet. Pulling my coat tighter to guard against the cold that seemed to seep into my bones, I went looking for the exchange window to convert into French francs the few pesetas I had left. It was early, and the money exchange was still closed. I rang my friends' number, but nobody answered and I assumed that they were *en route*. The few people around me hurried about their business and I decided to sit for a while and wait. I prefer to travel by train when in Europe. The flight to Paris was just an overnight stop, and I was looking forward to the train ride to Belgium, where I was to continue my university studies.

I can meditate—or fall asleep if I want to—anywhere, whether it is in busy restaurants, or airplanes, or waiting rooms. Temporarily delayed at the airport, and having nothing better to do at the moment, I fell asleep. After a few minutes, a gentle voice calling my name, and a hand on my shoulder woke me up. I found the face that woke me vaguely familiar, but not those of the other two women. They told me that my ride could not make it, as the car was broken down on the road to the airport. After a few more words of conversation, I learned that the women were not there to replace my ride to Paris, but to take me, if I agreed to go, to the Languedoc-Rousillon region in the South of France, land of my origins.

I was curious as to who these women were and how and why they knew me. They had an air about them that made me think of nuns, but they were not nuns and were not part of any church or religious group. They were certainly independent because they didn't belong to a larger body, but they were not part of the Independent Movement or any other known tradition. They told me that, according to their lore, their sisterhood had developed alongside Christianity since pre-Nicene creed times. Whatever the truth of their origin, their small group maintained safety in obscurity, probably since at least medieval times. They claimed a lineage direct from Mary Magdalene, one that had initiated or ordained only women for safety's sake, but not because they felt there was any impediment to ordaining men. Among their heritage, they possess a number of texts attributed to Joseph of Arimathea, Mary Magdalene, John the Disciple, and other later writers. I had never heard of them, but everything they were telling me sounded very natural and familiar, and I had no doubt of their authenticity.

They called their tradition *Le Saint Ordre de Marie-Madeleine*, which I rendered into English as "The Holy Order of Miriam of Magdala," but that's just a name to tell a first timer like me. Their lineage is transmitted through the breath and the imposition of hands in a ritual of extreme simplicity that, although mostly different in wording, context, format, and protocol, parallels the ordination of priests and consecration of bishops. No one can apply to study with them, as they are not known except among those initiated by them. They invite a woman only after she has been under observation for a number of years. Their purpose is mainly to keep that tradition and unbroken lineage alive. There can only be one active hierophant—or bishop—at a time, plus two others inactive, in case that *La Grande Dame* or, in English, "The Lady," dies without naming a successor.

No candidate, including me, had ever known of the Order's existence prior to their first contact. I accepted their equivalent of ordination and consecration at their hands as well as, at that time, becoming—in spite of, or because of, my young age—both the successor to *La Grande Dame*, or Madame (The Lady), and their seventh and last Marashin, a title given every few centuries and with no counterpart in other traditions. The only condition they asked of me was a solemn vow to never reveal their names, exact locations, or the fact of my own ordination, except under certain specified circumstances.

The Mary Magdalene lineage cannot be understood or studied in the same manner as the other fifteen traditional lines of apostolic succession to which I later became heir. To this day, the Order and their heritage remain partially secret. Even in our more progressive times there is still danger, and the protection of the identity of the others is still necessary were there to be an open resurgence of hostility toward women in spirituality. Bearing that in mind, for the past few decades I have been slowly working on an accessible, meaningful, and modern rendition of portions of their texts into the English Language. These are not yet available for publication, but they have been incorporated into our lectionary. Because of these constraints, I present this tradition as a mythological communion rather than as a historical curiosity, thus preserving its continuity and essence.

Mary Magdalene has for centuries seized the imagination of writers and story tellers, inspiring many legends and stories in France and elsewhere. Some, if not most, of them are quite meaningful and effective in stirring our psyches. I must say at this point, for the sake of clarity, that the Order and its teachings bear no resemblance to any modern popular work of fiction or speculative version of history, no matter how beautiful, exciting, or inspiring: no *Holy Blood, Holy Grail* and no *Da Vinci Code*-type of story; no marriage to Jesus, no child of Jesus, and certainly no Merovingian descendants; nothing that glamorous.

Nowadays, it is difficult to understand how a teenage girl can go to an undisclosed, secret location with three women she has just met for the first time. We must keep in mind that, in those times, hitchhiking was common and many Europeans my age traversed the Continent in their student years depending on the kindness of strangers. Call it trust, naïveté, or being nineteen, but that's not it. I had the previous year escaped from a political prison in a Communist country, where I had been interrogated and tortured in an unspeakable manner for a month. I had stared into the eyes of cruelty and sadism, all done for the sake of an ideology, so to say that I was naïve is just inventing a reason after the fact. I know how and why I believed them and went with them, but there is no way I can explain it in words. The memory of the experience is vivid, but it doesn't translate into sentences that can satisfy even me. I have been asked many times, and each time I have tried, to the best of my ability, to answer with details, but I become tongue-tied whenever I try. (Is it finger-tied when trying to write it down?) All I can say is that with tremendous trust and recognition of the heart, I went with them. A few days later, I continued my journey, carrying a precious secret in my heart that would remain so for over a decade. I arrived in Belgium right before my twentieth birthday.

It was not until eleven years later that I was contacted by Gnostic bishop Stephan Hoeller and ordained within Independent Catholic lines of apostolic succession.

In those intervening years the basis of my present work began to emerge, although I didn't know it then. I kept contact with my spiritual sisters in France, secretly and uninterrupted. My spirituality remained then as it is still today, experiential rather than based on belief. Meanwhile, I continued studying and reading. I left behind a path leading from international law to a possible career in diplomacy or with the United Nations to my real interests. Those ranged from astrophysics to medicine and included political science, philosophy and theology, Hinduism, with which I had been familiar for a long time, the teachings of Buddha, Sufi mystical poetry, and Jewish mysticism, especially Kabbalah. This last I had been familiar with since childhood, having had a Jewish grandfather knowledgeable on the Kabbalah who introduced me to the works of Isaac Luria (a 16th century Jewish mystic) and one of my beloved spiritual mentors.

I immersed myself in the works of Dominican theologian Meister Eckhart (*c.*1260-1327), whose works had been subject to an inquiry for heresy. He wrote of the *scintilla animae*, or "spark of the soul," which enables us to know God. The year after Eckhart's death, twenty-eight of his theses were condemned as heretical and, to this day, he has not been reinstated. There is no denying the resonance I found in his works and my own as yet undeclared, but already very clear, theological stance.

Another of my adopted spiritual mentors was Jesuit priest, paleontologist, and theologian Marie Joseph Pierre Teilhard de Chardin. In Teilhard I also found a kindred soul in which my love for science and evolution, coupled with a belief in a cosmic destiny for the species, was so elegantly developed in what he called "cosmogenesis." Rather than a duality of matter and spirit, he saw two dimensions of one reality. Everything in the universe, including human beings, is interconnected and bound together in a wholeness of unity. It is not the spirit that needs to evolve, but the evolution of the cosmos depends on the awakening or spiritualization of matter, and God is the Omega Point, the culmination of the cosmic process. Teilhard's two passionate loves were God and the universe, and he dedicated his work and life to integrate the two. He wrote under the constant accusations of heresy, which caused him much pain. His friend Père Pierre LeRoy said of Teilhard, "His own faith was in the invincible power of love: men hurt one another by not loving one another. And this was not naiveté, but the goodness of the man, for he was good beyond the common measure."

Enthralled in the work of these two giants as well as occupied with the rest of my studies and personal life, I still continued finding solace and kinship in the poetry of Saint John of the Cross, my constant spiritual mentor since early childhood. It is interesting to me that my three heroes in Christianity had been either suspected or accused of, or their work condemned as, heresy within their lifetimes. A word that has been long used in connection with my views and the one title that I wholeheartedly embrace is heretic.

At some point, I came across some extant works from the early Gnostics and immediately recognized in them kindred spirits. Except for some forms of Gnosticism, such as those derived from Manichaeism and Marcionism, most Gnostics were far from the world-hating dualists described by those who try to study Gnosticism strictly academically and externally, without having experienced it, vainly attempting to dissect the flavor of a fruit that they have never tasted or even seen. Gnostics spoke in myth and symbol and within the *mentalité* of their time. Gnosis comes from the Greek *gnosis*, meaning "knowledge"—not book-learning nor a knowledge that can be passed on to another, but a direct, mystical experience in a dimension not touched by chronological time. That describes exactly my own first hand familiarity with the Ineffable.

## Chicago

An invisible magnet that seemed to pull me toward San Francisco or somewhere near San Francisco brought me from Europe to the United States, but circumstances kept me in Chicago for a few years. This proved essential to laying the foundation of my present work and for establishing lifelong friendships. During my stay in Chicago, I was initiated in the Ramakrishna Order of Vedanta, another of my spiritual loves being Hinduism, especially the teachings of Sri Ramakrishna and Swami Vivekananda, the founder of Vedanta in the United States.

A few friends and I used to meet several evenings a week at informal gatherings where we shared bread and wine in the transformative magic of a naturally occurring Eucharist, a celebration of friendship and spirit in which we were fully humbled in gratitude toward a Benevolent Power that was almost palpable. We met in parks, at each other's flats, by the shores of Lake Michigan, and in restaurants. I could not speak of my ordination in the tradition of Mary Magdalene, but that was not necessary. In the heart of the Mystery such formalities don't matter. We could only acknowledge and bow to that Mystery to which we had been dedicated. My friends were Catholic, Protestant, Liberal Catholic, New Age, and occasionally Hindu. They were all men, not on purpose, but by happenstance.

We were all students, and money was scarce, but whenever we could we would meet in restaurants that were then inexpensive, such as those found in Chicago's Greek town. With glasses of Roditis, pita bread and flaming plates of Saganaki, the traditional dish of Greece made with kasseri cheese, we met in holy company, laughing, joking, and being fully holy and fully human, without pretense. This was where the food and the wine, our bodies and our souls, would awaken to the awareness that we are the sacred body and the royal blood.

In those informal *Aagapae*, the eternal priesthood latent within each participant shone like pin-point stars emerging inside the transparent enclosure of our mystical silence, where the hubbub of lively restaurants gently surrounded us as if from a distant dimension. Those meeting places were our temples, where the aliveness of the moment transformed all things. Even after having had a church for many years, I have always continued to practice a form of nomadic spirituality.

## California

By the time I moved to California, I was familiar with the Liberal Catholic Church and some other offshoots of Catholic, Anglican, and Orthodox groups, as well as with a couple of Old Catholic bishops of the Utrecht Succession. In several conferences, I spoke in favor of the ordination of women, although it never occurred to me to seek ordination myself, as I felt I had ordination enough in the Mary Magdalene tradition. Moreover, I never felt I needed the first ordination. Something had happened earlier in my life to which nothing could be added or taken away. I will speak of that in more detail later, when I get to the beginning.

In the latter part of 1973, I received a letter from a bishop whom I had never met, as with the Mary Magdalene priests in France. Dr. Stephan Hoeller, a Gnostic bishop of long standing and with a known affection for the Holy Sophia, the feminine aspect of God, had for some time been interested in opening the priesthood to women. He had heard of me through various sources and, after discussing his plans with three other bishops, wrote me a letter extending an invitation to ordain me within the traditional lines of apostolic succession. This was before the Episcopal Church began ordaining women.

What an opportunity to open the door for women to be accepted as priests! And a *Gnostic* bishop, at that! I meditated on the offer for a few weeks and consulted with Madame (The Lady) in France. She reminded me that in the oaths of secrecy I took, there was one clause. That when the time came, I would have the option to lift the veil of secrecy surrounding their existence, as long as I remained discrete as to names and exact locations.

Furthermore, she reminded me that my vow required me not to openly divulge my ordination unless and until I became publicly ordained through the traditional lines of succession. I was struck by the significance of the offer, and that same day called Bishop Hoeller to discuss the possibility with him.

What Groucho Marx said about marriage (i.e., "Marriage is a wonderful institution...but who wants to live in an institution?") can be aptly applied to my attitude toward any institution. Religions—mainstream as well as independent—tend to become institutions. While I love attending services in many of them and participate in their rituals, and many of them are worthwhile and even essential, I don't want to live in one.

A strange statement for a bishop with Independent lines of apostolic succession, but I see no conflict in this. The ordination would carry no expectations and have no strings attached, and I would remain fully independent and answerable only to God. At that time, I had no plans to start a church, for while being profoundly spiritual, I am not religious in the traditional meaning of the word. Had it been otherwise, I would still be serving today with the same passion and dedication, but in a different format.

I met +Stephan for the first time at the time of my ordination. Assisted by three other bishops and in the presence of witnesses, +Stephan ordained me in a moving ritual at his Chapel of the Holy Sophia in Hollywood, California, on January 19, 1974. Thus, I embraced the role of "ecclesiastical guinea pig."

## Founding of the Church of Gnosis (Ecclesia Gnostica Mysteriorum)

In 1978, I started a Gnostic Church in Palo Alto, California, and I named the chapel "Sanctuary of the Holy Shekinah." We remained at that location until April 1, 2007, when we moved to a larger building in Mountain View.

On January 18, 1981, seven years after my ordination by +Hoeller and with the same terms agreed at ordination, I was solemnly consecrated bishop at our Sanctuary of the Holy Shekinah in Palo Alto. Bishop Stephan Hoeller presided, assisted by the same other three ordaining bishops.

Once I was consecrated bishop in the traditional lines of succession, I began admitting men and women to the priesthood of both lineages. I believe that both traditions, being fully Gnostic, complement each other in my work.

In 1982, I returned to France with two traveling companions. During that visit, as a full successor of The Lady, the identities of every sister initiated were made available to me, as was the rest of that heritage. In the same manner, they keep in their records the names of each candidate that I ordain to the Order.

Before I began regular public celebrations of the Eucharist in 1978, a vision began to emerge that culminated in the foundation of the Sanctuary. It took the form of a spiritual shelter for travelers on the spiritual path—a small temple of the Mysteries, an outpost of the Divine, a sovereign territory on this planet for those longing to awaken and keep awake while in physical form.

I surrendered to the internal promptings in the only manner I could and still remain authentic to myself and the vision. I could not follow any external modes. I envisioned a sanctuary that I myself would like to attend, one with no membership, beliefs or dogma—a refuge for spiritual travelers, where no one would impose their reality upon another.

Our liturgy, while following a certain familiar order, is inclusive and thoroughly Gnostic, with our own music written specifically for our ritual. While I respect and honor the robes of my grandparents, I do not wear them, so we developed our own liturgy, mostly composed of texts from the Gnostic Gospels, the secret writings of the Mary Magdalene Order, and my own writings and prayers. All are welcome to communion regardless of gender, sexual orientation, religious background, or any other labels. The diversity of our congregation mutually enriches us.

Our priests manifest their vocation not only mystically, internally, and at the altar, but also in the world. Each of us serves according to our calling and talents. Some work with prisoners or in drug rehabilitation, some are dedicated to animal welfare, and others are involved in social justice. My particular form of praxis is spiritual direction, especially working with men diagnosed with AIDS. We don't work in the name of the church and usually not through organizations; in my case, it has been by word of mouth. We prefer to serve in quietness and humility.

My contact with those religious leaders of independent and mainstream bodies I have met has always been from cordial to warm, friendly and supportive. I also live in a part of the United States where diversity is more accepted than elsewhere.

Gender has not been a problem in my work, although

I can't swear as to whether it has been a problem for others. I feel just as comfortable with men as with women, perhaps because I don't think of myself in terms of gender. In truth, I don't see myself as a woman, but as a spark of the Divine in a human body. Those descriptions are useful to operate in the world, but they are absolutely meaningless in the Ultimate Reality that we in the West frequently call God.

## The Beginning

All stories should have a beginning, although when mine began is not exactly clear. Since my earliest recollections, from before I ever heard the word God, I can only tell of being carried in the flow of the Mystery, without question or resistance. I'm talking about being in my crib, through my toddler years, while learning to talk and walk and then begin reading at the age of three.

When I began to speak, my mother would ask me who I was talking to when she'd hear me say, "Don't ever, ever, let me forget." That was my first conscious prayer. I couldn't have told you then, had I had the words, what I under any circumstance could not afford to forget. There are no words for it, except that since the very beginning I have felt a sense of Presence—a love so utterly fulfilling; such an all-encompassing embrace that went even beyond Presence, for then there was no more presence, no division between that and "I," only an awareness of Oneness and of being outside of time. And then, I would return from the Oneness, but filled with a sense of trust and safety and the lingering taste and flavor of the Divine Beloved, who with His kiss forever stole my heart.

## Today

My work and existence are all one. There is no separation between God and non-God. Although I still dedicate at least one hour daily for meditation, I can't really say I meditate, for there is no "I" involved in this.

The rest of the time, my relationship with God remains one of lover and Beloved rather than of Parent-child. This is reflected in our liturgy. I did not choose this type of spiritual relationship. It just is. This is best described in Daniel Ladinsky's ecstatic renditions of the Sufi poet Hafez:

> *Throw away all your begging bowls at God's door,*
> *For I have heard that the Beloved*
> *prefers sweet, threatening shouts,*
> *Something on the order of:*
> *"Hey, Beloved,*
> *my heart is a raging volcano of love for you.*
> *You better start kissing me*
> *Or... else."*

In concluding this article, the spiritual fragrance of my many spiritual mentors gathers around me—their voices softly rising in a harmonious choir that envelops me with their warmth and gentle guidance, each voice a unique hue and quality, all blending, rising and falling in a haunting cosmic melody—their power to awaken undiminished by having left this earth, most of them long before this body was born. The keynote emphasizing the universal constant that reveals our underlying unity proves the same now as it ever was millennia ago: the phenomenon of waking consciousness is always and everywhere the same. It is universal and spans all ages and traditions. It does not matter what holy names, if any, we invoke; it does not matter what liturgies we use or what beliefs we have. It remains a universal unifying constant underlying this mixture of apparent disparate and opposing elements. We are drawn together to reveal that the movement toward the One is an inexorable one: bright, incandescent, and transforming. Behind all these words and doings, there is a sacred emptiness in which God—if I may use that term—flows like a rushing river. It is in that emptiness that I feel totally fulfilled. It is the ending of me.

The Most Rev. John Plummer, PhD

Mission Episcopate of the Theophany

# "One of Many Paths"

I WAS BORN ON CHRISTMAS DAY, 1968 in the small city of Bowling Green, Kentucky. My parents lived in Russellville, not far west from Bowling Green, where my father worked as a large animal veterinarian. Due to their recent swap from Methodist to Baptist, I successfully avoided infant baptism and remained a perfectly heathen baby. I wasn't even subjected to the Baptist rite of "child dedication" until after my brother was born in 1971. By this time we had moved to the suburbs of Nashville, Tennessee. The lack of sacramental ritual in our life did not indicate a lack of religious fervor. My parents were conservative evangelicals, with a fundamentalist approach to biblical interpretation. My mother read to us from the Bible every night. Years later, I still have large parts of the King James Version rolling about in my memory. My father was a deacon. There was no drinking, swearing, gambling, or other frowned-upon practices.

When it came to church, I was a cynical and questioning child, although with an underlying anxiety about my salvation. Every church service and every preacher we watched on television ended with a syrupy yet vaguely threatening appeal to sinners to give their hearts to Jesus. There was no small amount of subtle pressure to do so. At a Billy Graham crusade in Nashville in 1979, I walked the aisle to commit myself to Christ. From this distance in time, it is very difficult to sort out parental and peer pressure, the heightened emotions of the moment, and genuine religious experience. I had to repeat the walk on a Sunday at church, not long thereafter, followed by a conversation with the pastor which was intended to lead toward baptism and church membership. Let's just say the conversation didn't go well, and I was pronounced unready for the next step. I clearly remember my 10-year-old self walking out of the church building with an iron-willed determination to do my best not to go back. I never had another conversation with that pastor regarding baptism, and I spent my teen years avoiding church and Sunday School whenever possible.

At the same time that I was pushing away from the religion of my childhood, I began reaching in new directions. I became insatiably curious about the varieties of Christianity (and, later, the varieties of religious expression) and the history thereof. I read all I could from the library and the encyclopedia in our house. I was particularly drawn toward ritual and sacramental forms, prior to having any experience of them. I first participated in liturgical worship in a visit to a Missouri Synod Lutheran parish, and first saw a mass at the Roman cathedral in New Orleans on a family vacation, both during my high school years. I bought a copy of the *Book of Common Prayer*, but couldn't figure out exactly how to use it. I met a Roman priest, and, upon hearing of my attraction to his tradition, he gave me a crucifix which I wore for many years. From a directory of churches in the United States, I obtained addresses for some independent jurisdictions and orders, and proceeded to write to them. With a few, I had extended correspondence, but—perhaps mercifully, given my youthful naiveté—I never met any of their members or hierarchs in person.

By the time that I was a senior in high school, I was reading a lot of books on meditation, contemplation, and Catholic mysticism, especially Thomas Merton (along with gay novels!). I desperately wanted to be baptized in a sacramental church, and Rome seemed like the best option. My limited experience of Episcopalians had been confined to low-church evangelicals who seemed too much like what I was running from, the Orthodox churches were a mystery in all senses of that word, and the independents whom I had contacted were geographically far away. I decided that a Catholic college might be just the way to go.

Upon taking a tour of Fordham University in the Bronx, I felt immediately at home. Catholicism and the wild world of New York City in the mid-80s! Who says you cannot have it all? My years at Rose Hill were a wonderful time of exploration—theological, philosophical, political, magical, sexual, cultural—which continues to shape my life in many ways. I was received by the Roman church as a catechumen during Advent 1987, baptized at the Easter Vigil 1988, and confirmed a couple of weeks later. At my confirmation, Bishop Patrick Ahern said to me: "The world's your oyster, kid." And it was. The same people who led me on my journey of Christian initiation were also the friends and mentors on my other journeys of self- and world-discovery. I owe them thanks for showing me a holistic and life-affirming Christianity, unafraid of truth. I did not realize how rare this vision was.

In the midst of this whirlwind of Thomas Aquinas, Starhawk, anarchist political theory, Queer Nation, and the drag queens of the Pyramid, I made live contact with independent sacramental churches for the first time. One of the Fordham student newspapers printed a photograph of the sign for St. Michael's Liberal Catholic Church on East 53rd Street, humorously noting the conjunction of the words "liberal" and "Catholic." I immediately recognized the Liberal Catholic Church from my reading, and knew I had to visit. I took the subway into Manhattan on a February morning, to attend a Candlemas liturgy at St. Michael's. The parish then met in a small chapel on the second floor of the New York Theosophical Society building. The liturgy was splendid, and I returned many times. Following this first foray, I met a number of other independent communities and clergy.

While the Liberal Catholics and other independents suited my quirky and free-minded spirit, I wasn't quite ready to jump ship from Rome. I was a new convert, with the usual fervor, pursuing a degree in theology with a mind to a career as a priest, theologian, or both. I couldn't imagine leaving for a tiny church where I would be a volunteer, having to make a living in another way. After graduating from Fordham, I moved back to Tennessee to begin a joint MA/PhD program in "the History of Christian Thought" at Vanderbilt University.

Arriving at Vanderbilt, I found myself in a very different environment. Without changing my views, I went from being the heretical liberal of Fordham to being the orthodox Catholic of Vanderbilt. The liberal modern protestant environment pushed me closer to Rome, in reaction. I continued to explore vocational possibilities—diocesan priesthood, the Dominicans, and, most seriously, the Trappists. Of course, never content with a singular-path model, I also spent several years cultivating a relationship with the Shaker family at Sabbathday Lake, Maine (from whom I learned much, including an appreciation of the Divine Feminine as reality, not idea), attending twice weekly study groups devoted to the work of Austrian esoteric philosopher Rudolf Steiner, and following a number of my male ancestors through initiation into Freemasonry. The spiritual director assigned to me by the local Roman diocese probably thought I was mad!

With greater experience of typical Roman parish life in Nashville, and Roman diocesan leadership, I came to some realizations. I knew that as a Roman priest I would either be continually repressing myself (something I am not particularly good at), or I would be continually in trouble. I wondered if a contemplative, monastic priesthood would avoid at least some of the difficulty, and I went some distance in discerning a vocation with the Trappists. At a particular moment of crisis, I asked for counsel from local Baptist radical Will Campbell, who wrote me a very wise letter, which I still have, reminding me that if I am not free, then I will always have a problem.

So much for Roman priesthood.

After this series of closed doors, the year 1995 brought a conjunction of three influences which would shape much of my spiritual life to come. I discovered the British version of the "Western Mystery Tradition" especially through the work of Dion Fortune and Gareth Knight. After reading Knight's *Experience of the Inner Worlds*, I wrote him a fan letter. He replied and referred me a former student, Mark Nicholas Whitehead, who was living in the United States. I studied mysticism, qabalah, and magic with Whitehead for the next ten years. Roughly simultaneously, I managed to connect to the tradition of Paul Blighton and the Holy Order of MANS. The Holy Order had a presence in Nashville in my childhood, and I was fascinated by the brothers and sisters in clerical garb, whom we encountered primarily in the health food store. By the time I was old enough to investigate for myself, the Order had fractured, with the largest group (and the corporation) making its way into the Orthodox Church. I met some of the Orthodox ex-HOOMies at a theology conference, but I was looking for people who were openly continuing Blighton's initiatic work. In 1995, I made contact with Titus and Karen Hayden, who then were serving with the Science of Man Church, a continuation of Blighton's original, pre-Holy Order organization. I began studies in this tradition, which would eventually take me through several groups derived from Blighton's work— and, much more importantly, into a living experience of God which changed my life.

Again, around the same time in 1995, I decided I was going to find an independent catholic church with which I could work. By way of the internet (very new to me at the time), I located Bishop J.C. Catherine Adams and the Friends Catholic Community Church. The FCCC tried to combine Catholic sacramental life with Quaker spirituality and governance. I appreciated the freedom—although it also challenged me at times—and the fact that the church was openly ordaining women and LGBT persons. There was an FCCC community, St. Nicholas the Wonderworker, outside of Roanoke, Virginia, about seven hours away. I began driving back and forth to community gatherings in Virginia (also traveling to Maine and Colorado), journeying through the minor and then major orders. Together with my friend Larry Terry, I was ordained to the priesthood on November 9, 1996.

Following my ordination, I went through changes on many levels. Physically, I developed a strange skin rash, which resisted treatment until a capable spiritual healer helped me re-balance the energies running through my body. Mentally, I burned out on graduate school and signed up for a year in a voluntary service program which took me back to New York City. Emotionally, I began a new relationship with the person who would become my spouse. My frustrations with the Friends Catholic community led to my transfer to a sister jurisdiction, the American Catholic Community Church. While more stable, ACCC also had a stronger doctrinal focus and less place for esotericism, and thus with time became uncomfortable. My friend Larry, with whom I had been ordained, suggested that I be consecrated to free me to pursue an independent path.

Thus, on April 25, 1998, at the Oratory of the Little Way, a small Episcopal retreat house in Connecticut, I was consecrated by Catherine Adams, Larry Terry, Grace Franco, and John-Noel Murray. The consecration was not for any church, denomination, or jurisdiction, but solely for an independent mission episcopate. In the years that have followed, I have tried forming a connection to organized independent sacramental churches, and it has never gone well. I am sometimes a slow learner, but I gradually realized that I need to follow the spirit of my consecration, remaining free.

In many ways, it is the quest for a truly free sacramental priesthood, and the desire to help others along that path, which has defined my ministry since 1998. When I returned to work on my PhD in 2003, via the Graduate Theological Foundation, I changed my topic to an exploration of independent sacramental churches, primarily in North America. The results of my research were published in 2005 as *The Many Paths of the Independent Sacramental Movement.*

Having examined the background and present state of the independent movement, and having tried to articulate the ways in which we are knit together as a spiritual family, I have been more recently occupied with how we are called to move into the future. My later book, *Living Mysteries*, and a number of articles are my attempts to clarify my vision. I think it is important for us to look at how the Spirit is already present and moving in our midst, often precisely in the characteristics that we find embarrassing—small communities, physically solitary celebration of the eucharist, ordination of a high percentage of participants, and so on. If we look carefully, we may discover that we are being led into new, flexible, portable ways of being church.

I also continue to be engaged by the experiments of those who are finding ways into free, non-jurisdictional forms of priesthood, often outside of church structures altogether. In this, I have been particularly influenced by the vision of a "free priesthood" initiated by the Dutch-Australian priest Mario Schoenmaker, founder of the Church of the Mystic Christ. With people no longer coming to the priests and to traditional church settings, Mario resolved to send priests to the people, living and working out in the world.

Being a movement given to freedom and experimentation, I am sure we make plenty of mistakes, many of which will only become clear with time. However, I am equally sure that, even in our most bumbling and absurd moments, we are enveloped in the love of the One who is always working to set us free from all that binds us. I wouldn't have church any other way.

The Most Rev. River Sims

Society of Franciscan Workers

# "Blessed are the Poor in Spirit"

THE BEST SUMMARY FOR MY MISSION in life can be found in the statement: "Obedience to Christ does not consist in engaging in propaganda, nor even in stirring people up, but in being a living mystery. It means to live in such a way that life would not make sense if God did not exist."

On a warm January evening I was sitting with Charlie, my seventeen-year-old intern, as he interviewed me for a paper. The question was: "What qualifications must the director possess for this position?" I started to list my educational and vocational experiences, when Charlie interrupted. "River, cut the bullshit, what really makes you the skater-outlaw punk priest? What makes you able to be who you are to kids?" With insight Charlie raised a penetrating question.

Our education shapes us, and gives us the tools with which to look at those experiences in our lives that truly make us who we are. In looking back at the decades of my life I see a common thread that weaves through them. The thread of God's hand working through all the experiences, both positive and negative—nudging, guiding me into the path that I follow. For I have found that "in all things God works for good to those who love her."

The vocational path that I follow is that of living with homeless youth and sex workers on the margins.

My spiritual director once pointed out: "The people you serve are sitting in the middle of a highway with different trucks aimed at them—all the stereotypes, the biases of our society: drug addict, prostitute, thief, murderer, queer, transgender, bisexual, are aimed towards them and because you stand with these kids those trucks are aimed at you as well." And so I am identified with them, and treated as they are. And so why have I chosen this path? I believe it was chosen for me long ago, in my mother's womb, and the experiences of my life have led me to choose this vocation.

Two central threads which weave through my life are poverty and my commitment to vocation. I was born in poverty, and I have been poor in one way or another all of my life. Since a very young age I have understood God working in my life calling me to ordained ministry. My relationship to God has been the central relationship in my life since I was twelve. Like Paul, I find myself "working out my salvation."

What is poverty? It is not having the basic needs of life. But it is also feeling abandoned, alone, on the outside looking in, and not belonging.

My father left my mother before I was born. My mother was left pregnant, with no job. She returned to her parents' home in southeast Missouri, where she worked whatever job was available. It was hand to mouth. We lived in the projects, where poor people lived. At two my mother divorced my dad. When I was three my mother met a businessman, Wade Smith. He was a gentle man of faith, and a prominent and successful businessman. He fell in love with my mother, they were married, and he adopted me. My last memory of my biological father was at four. He came to sign the adoption papers, and I remember him picking me up, hugging me, and then driving away.

A child who loses a parent in those first five years through death or other means of separation has abandonment issues throughout his or her life. There is a sense of incompleteness, aloneness, and poverty.

From four onward I was raised in affluence with good parents. My parents loved me, my adopted father doted on me and saw me as his son. His side of the family never accepted me. They resented me, they resented my mother. The reason was simply money: we were his sole heirs. Only on my mother's side of the family was I accepted. And throughout my childhood and into early adulthood I suffered through a sense of rejection from my dad's family—I was never quite the real thing.

My family attended the local Methodist Church. I can remember until the day of his death my dad's first act of the morning was to read from the scriptures and pray. We attended worship every Sunday. The first Sunday of the month was the celebration of Holy Communion. When I was nine we were preparing for that celebration and my dad told me: "You can take communion but remember it is Jesus you are taking in." From that moment forward, the Eucharist has been the most special time, and I truly believed I was taking Jesus into myself. In that first communion Christ became a real being who touched my life. God became a living reality. And in these moments now, I am taken back to a camp-fire in the hills of Missouri when I was thirteen years old. It was a beautiful night in the foothills of the Ozarks and there was singing, skits, and finally the Eucharist. As I received the elements of the body and blood I remember the flicker of the flames as I found my heart strangely warmed. I knew without a doubt that was the One calling me, saying to me: "Follow me, and I will make you fish for people." There was a sense of knowing that, come what may, all would be well. As the years have passed the words "follow me" have summoned me through them.

From that time forward my vocational focus was the United Methodist ministry. I became deeply involved in the local church. The church for me became my home, it became where Christ is present. But beneath all of this there was a second force moving, my sexuality. I knew from the time I was ten that I was different: I liked boys. I was raised in a southern, Bible-belt environment and belonged to a denomination that had no tolerance of homosexuality. And so I kept all of this in. The years to follow were to be filled with depression and guilt. I believed very clearly that I was called to ministry, and so God must mean for me to be single and celibate. From all sides I was indoctrinated about the sinfulness of homosexuality.

I graduated from high school, began college, and took a student parish. I became the "perfect preacher boy." I played the game. I finished seminary and was ordained. I was placed on the "fast track," which meant I was being groomed for higher office. The church became my security blanket, and in some ways, my God. The church could do no wrong.

In seminary I was exposed to the Catholic Worker movement and to Dorothy Day. I fell in love with Dorothy, her theology, and her way of life. Throughout my pastoral ministry I was haunted, challenged by the discrepancies between my way of ministry and the theology of the Catholic Worker, which I believed was the way the Gospel was to be lived out. It haunted me that I made fifty thousand a year plus a nice house, and most of my members and surrounding community had far less. This too became a constant struggle in my life.

For fifteen years I was a United Methodist pastor. And for fifteen years I lived with guilt and depression, and played the game. And then I received a telephone call from a close friend of mine. He needed to see me.

We met at a coffee shop and as we sat down the tears flowed from his eyes. Sean was fifty, married with three grown children, pastor of a large church. Sean was the model of the perfect pastor. He shared with me that he was gay, had lived for many years with his wife in a brother/sister relationship, and would cruise the gay bookstores. Sean had been arrested that day in an adult bookstore for having sex with another man. His whole world was caving in, his career was over. In those moments I moved ahead twenty years and saw myself. I knew in that moment I had to be true to myself, to the church, and to my God.

I called my bishop and we met the following day. Thinking he would understand, and knowing I was celibate, I believed we would be able to work things out where I could have therapy and still pastor. My bishop, the man who once saw me as a son, gave me twelve hours to be out of the parsonage. I was placed on "Leave of Absence". I said to him: "The Discipline says if you are celibate and single, one is allowed in ministry if he or she is gay or lesbian or bisexual." He replied: "No gay man is celibate, and I have to be aware of the financial consequences for the church if you are coming out and serving a church." Within hours the word was out and my friends of many years shirked away. I found myself on the streets, friendless, and alone. The church that I trusted and served had turned its back on me. God, for all intents and purposes, turned his back on me as well. I was a sinner beyond the pale of grace.

I hired an attorney and began a lawsuit against the church for breaking my contract, but work was impossible to find. Later in the legal process we found that my supervisors in the church blackballed me. They wanted me gone. I was angry. And then one day I was reading the paper and saw this advertisement: Man to Man Escort Wanted, Good Money! And thus began my second career—male sex worker. Being a sex worker was a way for me to crash out, to explore my sexuality, and to give my finger to the church. It pleased me to no end to know that the money I used to sue them came from prostitution. The church became an institution that I did not want to be apart of. The grace I learned from that institution was not practised. I discovered that in a legal battle the Church could play dirtier than a secular entity.

I moved to Los Angles where I lived in Hollywood with punk kids. The punk scene became a place where I found myself accepted and loved for who I was. The music appealed to my rebellion against authority, and the acceptance of the community was the true grace. I made good money and used it for the lawsuit and to go back to school for another Master's.

The lawsuit was settled. I could have returned to the ministry, but instead surrendered my ordination. I wanted nothing to do with the institutional church. Even in the darkness, and the chaos of that time there was always God. I could never run away from God and her nudging. But I stayed away from anything that resembled institutionalized religion.

All my life I had been drawn to the liturgy of Catholicism. The symbolism, the mystery drew me. I was a "high church" Protestant. I was getting tired of prostitution. The excitement had run its course. The guilt surrounding a lot of the things in my work was affecting me. One day I was passing by the Cathedral and the door was open. I wandered in. As I gazed at the crucifix it was if the eyes of Jesus penetrated me, and I heard a voice say: "I knew you in your mother's womb, I called you, knowing who you are." I felt this presence of love and grace surround me. I knew I was loved, and so within a few weeks I walked away from being a sex worker, and got a job at Burger King. I finished my degree and began my third career: counsellor with homeless runaway kids in Minneapolis.

Those three years were great. While I stayed away from organized religion I continually explored the Biblical foundations of homosexuality and the seeds planted in seminary began to blossom. I began to see the Scriptures in a new light. In therapy I worked on all the guilt that surrounded my sexuality and my anger towards the church. I began to explore the Metropolitan Community Church and the United Church of Christ, but was turned off by the institutions.

In November of 1993 I attended a conference for therapists working with male prostitutes in San Francisco. I fell in love with the city. We were brought to Polk Street where the street hustlers hung out as a part of the conference. I was taken with the kids, and felt there was something I could do. During the previous three years I struggled with my love of the Catholic Worker. That struggle was that of a call. And I knew that first day on Polk Street I would return to do a Catholic Worker ministry.

I began putting out job applications, and then one day in September of 1994 I was offered a job as a case manager in Marin. I was there within a week, and by the middle of October had found a place on Polk Street. Within two years, I was no longer working a secular job. During the first year I "hung out" with the kids of Polk and the ministry began to evolve into a ministry of presence. But once again I experienced a nudging within me. There was a need for a sacramental ministry among them. I had always known I was called to ordained ministry, but vowed never to return to the institutional church. An Episcopal bishop friend of mine suggested I look at an independent denomination, the Evangelical Anglican Church in America. He believed that the independent movement was less institutional and would allow me to do ministry in the way I was called. And so I approached their bishop, went through the process and was ordained a priest in October of 1995. While the independent movement was a good fit allowing me to practice ministry as I was led, there was still the reality that my call to the margins was not one that resonated with my colleagues in the ministry, especially bishops. I am one who walks a different path, who sees the margins as where Christ is most present. Independent bishops often duplicate what those in the mainline churches represent—the need for recognition, institutionalization. Rather than put new wine in new wine skins, new wine is often placed in the old wine skins. This lead me through three different groups, each time leaving over what I see as a conflict of theological perspective—a theology of the margins versus a theology of the institution. Throughout this journey I continued to meet people like myself, living and working on the margins, called to ordained ministry, but unable to fit into the mode of the institution. During this period I felt nudged once again, nudged to be present to those who do ministry on the margins, to be the church to them. And so I followed the suggestion of a bishop friend and responded to the call of being elevated to the episcopacy. On October 4, 2007, at Grace North Church in Berkeley, California, I was consecrated a bishop, whose ministry is to those who work with people on the margins. The independent movement is a good fit to the way in which I practice ministry, and also to my living on the margins. The church is the body of Christ, individuals who are Christ to others. They are those who surround me each week on the street when I celebrate the Eucharist, they are those who work with me on the streets and share the ministry of the streets with me.

Over the years my prayer life has been shaped by these events. My own personal experience through the years has taught me one significant lesson—when one moves away from the Center, he or she will move into the darkness, the chaos. I live in a world of sex and drugs. And I see on a daily basis what happens when people have no Center, nothing to give them meaning. I am well aware that unless I stay centered in Christ I move into my own shadow of depression, cynicism, and burn out. People are often surprised when they come to the Eucharist I celebrate, how traditional it is. They assume because I am who I am it will be "way out there." For me, the Center is found in the liturgy, the Eucharist. It is what holds everything together, and from which all ministry flows. We serve a meal after the Eucharist. For me it is symbolic that from the Great Banquet flows the Works of Mercy. Our lives become the Eucharist as we move to the streets. The Liturgy of the Hours grounds my daily prayer life. Praying the Psalms remind me that the questions humanity struggles with have been the same questions for human beings from the beginning of time, and in the center is God.

And so for me poverty in its many forms has brought me to the knowledge that only in dependence on God is there real security.

People ask why I came to Polk Street, and my answer is to meet Christ. The words "Follow me" have summoned me through the years. I have been praised, condemned, rejected, but always I am summoned by those words. My dreams of large churches have come down to sitting on the couch with twenty-two-year-old Daniel, whom I have known since he was fifteen. Daniel has floated in and out of my life these years, always maintaining a connection. This night he has been using heroin, talking of his death. All I can say is: "Daniel I have loved you as long as I can remember, and will love you always, and if something happens to you a part of me will die as well." He smiles with tears in his eyes, leans over and kisses me on my cheek and says: "Don't worry, I will be alright," and he leaves. This is where that call so long ago has led me, the streets of San Francisco, with a group of rag tag kids, in whom I find Jesus. For this night on my couch sat Jesus in the flesh, in all of his pain and crucifixion. *Deo Gratias!* Thanks be to God!

The Most Rev. Professor
Elizabeth Stuart SSB

Archbishop of the Province of
Great Britain and Ireland, Liberal
Catholic Church International

# "I Am Still Learning"

THERE ARE FOUR STATUES on my mantle piece which I think neatly summarise the pilgrimage which has brought me to be a bishop in the Liberal Catholic Church International.

The first statue is of the Infant of Prague. It belonged to my maternal grandmother, a fiery woman of Irish descent and for me represents my solidly Roman Catholic upbringing. I was brought up a Roman Catholic in the South East of England in the 1960s in a very traditional parish resistant to the changes of the Second Vatican Council. It was a cultural Catholicism of processions, queues for confession, benediction, rosary, May devotions, and the Holy Souls. I found a tremendous sense of identity and freedom in it. I have never experienced Catholicism as personally oppressive. I knew there were things wrong with it from an early age but I always believed that change was possible. My mother had a healthy suspicion of over the top piety and my father was not a Catholic, so religion was an essential part of our life but not heavy or forced. It was a mystical Catholicism of incense, Latin, patron saints, angels, novenas, scapulars, pilgrimages, and miracles. The veils between worlds were thin. I have seen this type of Catholicism being slowly eroded in Britain to be replaced by a bland, flat, emaciated form without any cultural carry-over. The Catholicism of my youth raised questions about the instability of gender. I was taught by nuns with male names, who I had to address as sister or mother even though they were not related. I was allowed to take a male name, Augustine, at confirmation. Liturgical dress challenged notions of maleness and femaleness too. And of course, I was probably the last generation for whom celibacy and the religious life was held up as an ideal. I experienced the religion of my youth as a rich, radical tradition.

I have had a vocation to priesthood for as long as I can remember. I can have been no more than six years old when I had a dream I was celebrating Mass, eastward facing, at a side altar in my parish church. I used to play at being a priest which worried my parents because, in those days, a woman priest was a nonsense and they came, I think, to see my sense of vocation as somehow unnatural. So as I grew up I had to stop acting it out. I never lost that sense of vocation but I channelled it into academic study. Forty years after that childhood dream I found myself celebrating Mass at a side altar in a Roman Catholic retreat center. When I turned around to give the final blessing, I noticed that my congregation included a load of seminarians and a cardinal!

Beside the Infant of Prague stands a statue given to me

by a friend who walked the pilgrim route to Compostela. The statue is of a woman pilgrim, stout, with backpack and in full stride, leaning on her staff as she walks. I love this figure. For me the Christian life is a pilgrim life, a constant striving after and towards God. We are dealing with what the poet R.S. Thomas called "a fast God," always ahead of us, always leading and teasing us on. To think you have arrived, to imagine that you have caught God is perilous, it is the foundation of religious fanaticism and intolerance. Like the theologian Origen, I expect my pilgrimage to God to take me through many worlds beyond this. A key stage in my pilgrimage was when I had to move from a convent school to a grammar school for my last years at school. Here I was able to study theology as an academic subject with complete intellectual freedom. From school I went to study theology at Oxford and was lucky enough to be taught by some great men (they were all male) including G.B. Caird, J.C. Fenton, John Macquarrie, Kallistos Ware, and others, and went on to do my D.Phil there. I was trained at Oxford in Liberal Theology, and demythologisation was the chief approach. And that is what I taught when I left there to take up an academic post. At this time theologies of liberation were just beginning to impact British theology and I embraced these with enthusiasm. I have been able to make a small contribution to the development of gay and lesbian theology and feminist theology, as theologies of liberation.

But even when I was fully immersed in these movements for liberation, I was uncomfortable with their reductionist attitude to faith, their rejection of the transcendent horizon, and lack of sense of mystery. I became increasingly uncomfortable with all this as the years went on.

At several points I considered offering myself for ordination in other churches but I ultimately could not compromise on two issues: inclusivity and catholicity.

I also became increasingly aware that liberal and liberationist theologians had just conceded the tradition to conservatives. And this brings me to my third statue, a statue of St. Brigid of Kildare. I attended a feminist theology conference in Ireland and went on an excursion to Kildare. There I learned of St. Brigid and the tradition that she had been ordained a bishop, her theology of radical hospitality, and her ambiguous relationship with Rome. I began to explore this tradition and discovered that it contains discourses and memories more radical than anything created by contemporary theologians. Much of my own work has been about the recovery of the ancient Christian valorisation of friendship as the ideal relationship which provides a radical counterpoint to the contemporary Christian discourse on marriage and family life.

A key point in my pilgrimage on this route was a meeting in the late 1990s I attended in Lambeth Palace hosted by the then Archbishop of Canterbury. It was a meeting of theologians gathered to discuss homosexuality. All sides of the debate were represented and a good natured and deep discussion took place. But I suddenly realised during the course of that day that theologies based upon experience are only useful as an empowering exercise among a particular group of people. The men and women gathered around that table had such vastly different experiences that they simply could not enter into each other's experience, however hard they tried. The only thing these people had in common was the Christian tradition and its language and grammar. I knew then that the only hope for any resolution of this issue lay in the tradition. I also became aware that theologies based upon experience almost always end up doing violence to the experience of those who do not conform to the majority and I became uncomfortable with this aspect of my own work. So I began a new phase in my own theological development which involved a radical critique of my own earlier work as well as an immersion in the Christian tradition.

What I found in the Christian tradition was teaching which set the whole sexuality debate on its head. I found the belief that gender is not ultimate; in Christ there is no male and female. Jesus is born of no male matter, the product of the Shekinah overshadowing the Virgin and producing a humanity in which gender does not define a relationship with God and therefore should be of no concern to us. I came to understand that we had all rather missed the point and were preoccupied with fighting a battle which had been won in the great drama of salvation. From a theological perspective, gender and sexuality do not exist. All that exists is desire and the issue is whether that desire can be rightly ordered towards God, either through the prism of marriage or through the prism of monasticism (both defined widely). I have always had enormous respect for the vowed celibate life but I came to see it as having enormous significance in reminding us that all desire has its only and true end in the divine. A Church which has no vowed celibates is in danger (as is recently very evident) of collapsing discipleship into marriage, family life, and the current social order.

Around this time Queer Theory as espoused by Judith Butler and others began to hit the academy. It seemed to me that the only community on the planet under a command to be queer, to perform gender in such a way as to subvert it, was the Church and indeed, this is what I had experienced as a child. I moved then from writing gay and lesbian theology towards developing a queer theology which proclaimed the liberation from sex, gender, and sexuality to all.

By this time I had been in a relationship for nearly twenty years. That relationship ended suddenly and, for me, unexpectedly, in 2001. In the same month as that happened, when I felt my life to be in ruins, I met a former Liberal Catholic bishop, Richard Palmer, who was at that point establishing a new province. I knew something of the Old Catholic tradition and Liberal Catholicism, having specialised in British Church history at Oxford. Bishop Richard presented me with a possibility I had never had before, namely to fulfil a lifelong sense of vocation without compromising on Catholicity or inclusivity. More than that, I was reintroduced to a Catholicism something like that of my childhood, with an emphasis on mystery and liturgy. I felt as though life had stripped my soul bare and that in its naked state, my vocation was exposed in such a way as to no longer be ignorable or repressible. I felt it was all I had left. I had my fears, about losing respect, about becoming involved in fringe groups and so on, but these fears did not overwhelm me and I said "Yes." I was put first into minor orders, then made deacon and finally priest, all in 2001. I found myself catapulted into a reality thicker than I had ever previously imagined.

This brings me to my fourth statue, a golden angel of African appearance whose face is raised upwards in bliss as if soaking up the warmth of divine grace. Remember that I had been trained in liberal theology, and deconstruction and demythologisation had been my chief theological tools. Queer theory/theology had reminded me that things are not always what they seem to be and reengagement with the tradition had taught me the value of a transcendent horizon. As a deacon particularly, I found myself immersed in the study of the angels. Deacons in traditional Catholic understanding share in the ministry of angels. I began to understand something of the interest that new age spiritualities have in such things and the shame that the Churches have lost a sense of the richness of the heavenly court. I also realised that developing a mystical sense was not without its dangers and only a very disciplined prayer life could keep one sane and properly spiritually fit for dealing with such matters.

All my adult life I have been a political activist. I remember the shock I felt when a fair few of my contemporaries suddenly abandoned activism all together and became Buddhist monks or nuns. Now I too found myself drawn into prayer as a kind of activism, as a way of reaching situations and people beyond physical contact. I discovered that prayer was not an activity but an orientation, a way of being, a consciousness of being in the divine life.

When ordained a deacon and then a priest the liturgy instructs you to pray for the living *and* the dead and I discovered once again a great concern and fellowship with the Holy Souls.

When I became a priest I found myself questioning one of the great "orthodoxies" of feminist theology; that the language of sacrifice is patriarchal and oppressive. I found myself caught up in the great sacrifice of the divine, the breaking open of the heart of God, not just in history but continually in the sacraments. I began to understand that love is sacrifice and no more and no less, the willingness to pour oneself out or to contract oneself for another. I also began to realise that the heart of the priest must be continually open to mediate that sacrificial grace.

Priesthood is a gender free state. I love the tradition of eastward facing altars where the priest leads the people towards the place of resurrection, their position and vestments obliterating gender. The practice of facing the people makes the gender and personality of the priest something to get past or through.

I believe that sacraments change the world making Christ present as really as he was in a stable in Bethlehem or on a cross in Calvary. I was ordained to assist in that miracle. I therefore see it as my obligation to celebrate Mass every day. I do not understand priests who do not do so. One is never alone—the angels, saints, and dead gather. Every other aspect of ministry can be performed by a lay person, the sacraments are our particular concern. A priest is a midwife of Christ bringing him to birth in a world which groans with longing for him. If all a priest did was celebrate Mass every day they would have fulfilled their priesthood.

On All Saints Day 2001 I founded—with Fr. Kevin Woodward—the Society of St. Brigid, a clerical order devoted to prayer and to following the example of St. Brigid in offering outrageous hospitality.

I was content and thought that all was now settled. I most certainly had absolutely no desire to be a bishop. I was now well enough inducted in Liberal Catholic thought to understand that a bishop is an open channel of grace and has not rest by night nor by day. I had also learned something of the idea of the seven initiations and seen bishops crucified. I knew that it would cause huge controversy and suspected that my job might be jeopardised. So when I was first approached about becoming a bishop in the Open Episcopal Church I literally ran away from the table. But I knew by now that however hard you run if God wants you he gets you in the end. I also knew that faith was actually about putting everything on the line and trusting that it would be okay. This was a test of my faith and so in the end I conceded. The fuss and the worry did come in bucket loads but, like my pilgrim statue, I set my face against the wind and walked forward. What I walked into I can hardly begin to describe. I now find myself a guardian of tradition, a custodian of the sacraments and dispenser of the grace of ordination. And I find myself drawn ever deeper into the thickness of reality. All I know is that this is nothing whatsoever to do with me in the sense that I have not earned it, I am not worthy of it, and I doubt God's good sense in choosing me to do it. I have also learned that the Holy Spirit only gets in through the cracks in our lives. It is our scars and wounds that are used more than our talents.

The Open Episcopal Church advanced a free Catholicism which allowed not only freedom of thought but also freedom of worship. As I found myself being drawn more and more into the mystical dimensions of Catholicism this lack of official liturgy and discipline became more difficult for me and in 2006 the OEC let me go, without rancour and with great love, so that I could be incardinated in the Liberal Catholic Church International, a Church which did not ordain women to the major orders until 2004. I am not a Church-hopper at all but I feel that I have somehow always been set on the path to Liberal Catholicism. The Liturgy is stunningly beautiful and I refuse to accept the arguments of those who claim it is not pastorally appropriate because it is too difficult to understand, too complex, etc. The whole point of the Christian life is to enter into the mystery of the incarnation, death, resurrection, and ascension of Our Lord, not to grasp it, not to understand it, but to live it, to be caught up in the divine dance of sacrificial love which has a splendour which can only be expressed in a beautiful liturgy. I like being under authority and subject to a discipline. These things to me are essential to the Christian life.

I have no idea what the next stage of my pilgrimage will be as I seek the place of my resurrection (as the Celtic Christians used to say) except that I now find myself seeking solitude to pray and study. I am on the lookout for a hermitage for when I retire from academic life. When I was ordained a priest I took a vow of celibacy. I have known the joys and pains of a relationship but I felt clearly called to the celibate life when I began down the path of ordained ministry. For me celibacy is about learning to love divinely, that is, sacrificially. Of course being celibate has no effect on desire nor does it stop one falling in love or being lonely. It is a hard school in which one tries to learn to take these things to their true end. Inevitably there is failure as there is in a marriage but, in both, faithfulness is the key, sticking with it even when you cannot bear it anymore.

Friendship, which has always been important to me, has become even more so. Loneliness is the chief demon of the vowed celibate. I am lucky to have companionship which keeps the demon mostly at bay. My closest friend is an uncompromising atheist and holds very different political views to me as well. I think it is vital to have people close to you who challenge you at every turn. The fact is that religion can turn perfectly nice people nasty and nasty people into homicidal maniacs. For many people religion is not good for them. They take it too seriously in the sense that there is no room for doubt in their lives. A life without doubt is a life without faith. The only way that faith can redeem itself from this tendency towards fanaticism and intolerance is through continual self-questioning and admitting room for doubt. We may be wrong. I may have wasted my life in peddling illusion and delusion. That is a fact that I should never forget and I am grateful that I am not allowed to!

As a bishop I am probably quite demanding. I expect my priests to say Mass daily and all other ordained ministers to say the offices each day. I believe that clerical dress is sacramental. It reminds the cleric that they are set apart and belong primarily to Christ and it makes them visible and available to others. This, of course, has its dangers and risks but clerics should be willing to risk everything. I also expect my clergy to engage in some sort of study. I have a plaque on my mantle piece, it quotes Michelangelo and reads, "I am still learning." Constant study keeps the mind open to the Holy Spirit and guards against complacency and narrowness.

I strive to represent and incarnate a Catholicism which is an expression of the life of God: generous, all-embracing, hospitable, diverse, and yet focused in the sacraments. That is what Catholicism is to me and what I understand myself to be charged to defend and pass on.

The Most Rev. Alexis Tancibok

Grace Catholic Church

# "The Mission Continues"

I NEVER WANTED A MITRE. I had no such ambition. My calling, as I understood it, was to serve my community as a priest. My community, on the other hand, had a radically different idea of how I might serve. While I had grave misgivings about my own suitability, I was committed to serving the community as I had been asked. Thus, when elected, I felt I had no choice but to say yes. My approach not only to being chosen, but also toward my life in office, has been shaped by experiences both before my election and during my episcopacy. Moreover, during my fourteen years in office I have gained a greater appreciation for the (what I would say are unique) challenges to bishops and communities in our OC/IC context. In the following few paragraphs, I will offer a brief narrative of how I came to be here and will touch on a few of those themes that are part of our unique experience as Old and Independent Catholics.

I must say I do not trust those who, without being asked by their community, seek a mitre. When I worked in the bookstore of Virginia Theological Seminary, I observed numerous instances of ambitious clergy and seminarians mapping out their plans to "ensure" that they were bishops themselves within "X" number of years. They had met the right people, and sought placement in the right parishes and dioceses, so as to enhance the probability that they would quickly rise through the administrative ranks of the US Episcopal Church. What offended me in these conversations was that, while there were plenty of references to the prestige of a given diocese and the perks and pay on offer from particular congregations, there was no mention of the Gospel, the people of God, or serving Christ.

A few years before being elected bishop in my own community, I experienced what happens when bishops put their own personal agenda and issues before the needs of the community. The infighting of the three bishops and their factions in the first synod I joined, the Free Catholic Church International (FCCI), resulted in the dissolution of the community, caused untold hurt to members and created at least four new synods, including my own. The implosion occurred at what many of us now refer to as "the Synod from Hell" in June of 1993, when I had been a deacon since October of the previous year. We had, I seem to recall, around one hundred people attending that synod. They came from all over the United States to be together, to pray, to share fellowship, and to celebrate a number of ordinations. In the run up to the synod, however, one of our bishops abandoned Christianity in favour of an extreme, esoteric form of Gnosticism centered on what he called "the Great That." Our other two bishops could not, or would not (there was some debate as to which), stand up to their colleague and expel him from the church. Our community in Washington was comfortable pushing the traditional boundaries a bit, but we all recognised that there is a point at which one crosses the border into "another" spirituality that is not Christian. This particular bishop had done just that, and the community (and others in the church) said so. The gathering, which should have been a wonderful experience for us all, quickly disintegrated into the death throes of the church. At one point, the newly post-Christian bishop even accused me of practising black magic! I got off lightly—others, such as Catherine Adams (then an Archpriest), were horribly abused by the bishops in their struggle amongst themselves. Only bishops had full authority to act and make decisions in the FCCI, and the rest of the community was helpless to act. Only bishops, rather than the whole community, had the power to enforce the canons; this meant that if the bishops chose not to act, the community was effectively powerless to hold them accountable. Finally, neither of the other two bishops chose to undertake the necessary leadership to put the community first, protect the clergy and ministries entrusted to their care, restore order in the synod, and rebuild our confidence in them. Because there was no leadership and no structure in place to hold the bishops accountable, a church of over one hundred people disintegrated over three days.

My community, St. Mary Magdalene's in Washington, did not long survive the aftermath. For months afterwards we attempted to discern a way forward as a united group, but the balance of different spiritual disciplines and theologies had been disrupted and eventually we had to accept that there were now different groups emerging and moving in separate directions. During this period, Bishop Martha Schultz (d. 2007) consecrated Catherine Adams. Catherine then took on the mission of offering safe haven—support and Episcopal care—for individuals and communities affected by the dissolution of FCCI. My community was one of those that gladly accepted her offer.

As an aside, after my own consecration I thought it was only right to follow Catherine's example and offer episcopal support to clergy and groups in the wider OC/IC community, if called on to do so. My experience has been that the most difficult part of taking on such "refugees" is preventing them from imposing their particular values or spiritualities on the rest of the community. Ever since our community began, we have been a bi-ritual synod, enjoying the contributions of both Eastern and Western ideas and styles while celebrating our shared OC/IC identity. In 2007, however, we felt compelled to abandon this long-cherished tradition largely due to our experience of trying to provide a home for refugees, many forcefully attempting to impose a particular Western liturgy and style upon the rest of the community, and sometimes causing a great deal of confusion and hurt. While it is a lovely ideal to have a synod encompass as many ideas of being "church" as possible, I have learned that the ideal has a threshold—a point when differing sets of ideas and practices begin to compete with one another and at which that diversity is not constructive but destructive. Here is where OC/IC bishops can greatly benefit from being a friend to one another. We each express particular theologies and spiritualities of the Christian tradition. This is a wonderful element of our movement, one we ought to use to the advantage of the wider OC/IC community by introducing individuals and ministries who may not "fit" too well in our own community to bishops and communities that do share a similar vision. This would, I think, reduce substantially the instability experienced within the movement.

Turning back to my own narrative, we had just emerged from underneath the debris of the collapse of FCCI, we had acquired new communities, and together we were still finding our feet. So now, more than ever, I most certainly *did not* want a mitre. Thus, when the subject of my succeeding Bishop Catherine Adams was first raised within my community in late April, 1995, I was horrified and made it clear that I had no interest in being, nor desire to become, a bishop. So adamant was I that I ought not to be chosen, I worked with members of my local community, Sts. Cyril and Methodius in Washington, DC, to compile arguments from history and tradition in order to "dissuade" the wider community from considering me for the post. I was too young and inexperienced. I had only been ordained a few years. In our community at the time there were two other priests who were both older and more experienced in ordained ministry than I; one of them ought to be chosen, and not me. I believed (and still hold) that OC/IC communities are too quick to ordain and consecrate individuals—only to discover after it is too late that some were not ready and others were totally unsuited for such an office. I did not wish to become another example of this particular problem. We were glad of Bishop Catherine's pastoral care and protection. I for one was reluctant to surrender that little bit of stability. We needed more time. I knew that the day would come when it would be our turn to be shoved out of the nest, but surely that was sometime in the distant future. Catherine disagreed and believed that it was time for us to install our own "home-grown" leadership and become fully autonomous.

While the community accepted that there is a problem within the OC/IC community of consecrating candidates who are unsuitable, and often for the wrong reasons, my other arguments (that I had no ambition for a mitre, that I was too young and inexperienced, and that we were not yet ready to—or even ought not to—be autocephalous) failed to carry the day, and on 14 May, 1995, I was elected by an overwhelming margin, by our synod, to succeed Catherine Adams. (I was consecrated a month later on the 24th June, 1995 in Roanoke, Virginia.) When the result was announced, I was in shock. As the community applauded my election, I think I swore.

Episcopal election ideally is an act of the community bearing witness to the charism of the office already present in the individual chosen. Strictly speaking, it is at the urging of the Holy Spirit that the community elects someone to serve as bishop, and not some other influence. How it was that my community saw in me this "charism" I doubt will ever be clear to me. I most certainly did not! I was, at that time, only just coming to grips with what it meant to be a priest, a vocation I felt I had some active input in discerning whether or not I was truly called to. Now an elected and consecrated bishop, I had to start all over again.

There is, I think, a reason why the ideal practice for episcopal elections is an act of the community and not the individual. Any sane person who, as an outsider, sits and seriously contemplates a life in episcopal office would justifiably run and hide when asked to take on this role (according to legend some actually did). Where, I wondered, does one begin to learn how to be a good OC/IC bishop? The funny thing is that, with the exception of my experiences with Catherine Adams, I had only negative points of reference (mostly based on my experience in the FCCI). That is to say, I had ideas about what I did not want to see happen while I held this office. An apophatic role model of the episcopacy, however, is not really an effective one; it lacks something of the forward momentum needed to actually fulfil the community's expectations of what a bishop does.

My first point of reference for beginning to construct a base upon which I could build a model of episcopal ministry was my own family history. Over three generations, various members of my family have been (some still are) Old Catholic. I come to this life of faith with an understanding that why we do various things in our context is influenced by our OC/IC history. Already, by the time of my election, I had observed other OC/IC bishops making choices that seemed to be disconnected from what I knew of our history. For example, in the FCCI, the laity had almost no voice in the life of the synod. I knew from family experience of living in the Old Catholic tradition that this was not in keeping with one of the fundamental rationales for our movement. I felt I needed to have a better understanding of how situations like this came about and why it was still important for us now. I therefore took advantage of the library at the seminary where I worked and began in earnest to research the history of Old and Independent Catholicism. In the process of doing so, I not only gained a deeper understanding of part of my own personal history, but found inspiration and insight in the ideas, successes, and mistakes of the many historical figures of our movement.

My interest in our history has since gone beyond looking for examples of how to (or how not to) be an OC/IC bishop. I have acquired a passion for our history. In 1998, I studied Old Catholic history at Oxford for a term as part of an exchange program. It quickly became apparent that nearly all of the available resources about OC/IC history are at least 40 years out of date, and often written not by our own people but by biased observers. We needed a collection of the contemporary stories, recording the issues and ideas of our people, available to anyone who might want to do research or simply learn more about the movement as it is today. Thus, in 2007, I started the *Indie Voices Archive Project* (http://www.gracecatholic.net), a collection of oral history and video interviews telling the personal stories of people in the movement. Eventually, it will also include discussions on aspects of the theology and practice of the contemporary movement.

Exploring historical models of the OC/IC episcopacy led me to ask about the origins of the office, as well as its theology. For example, the nature of our individual communities leads others to describe us as embodying an "Ignatian model" of church, referring to St. Ignatius of Antioch's axiom: wherever the bishop is, the church is; wherever the church is, the bishop ought to be. I wondered how accurate was this description? What exactly did it mean in terms of theology? Did this model, or other late antique models, still have something fresh to contribute to our contemporary OC/IC way of life? Looking for answers to these questions had a big effect on the future course of my academic life—and that in turn affected the shape and direction of my episcopal ministry. Once I had completed my BA in philosophy and religious studies (1998), I moved on to complete an MA in Patristics at King's College, London (2000) and, finally, to start a PhD in late antique theology at the University of Durham (still in progress).

When I was consecrated I had not yet finished my first degree; indeed, I had been ordained to the priesthood in September, 1993 without a BA. I ran out of money halfway through my first attempt to get a degree at the University of Pittsburgh. My preparation for ordination was largely undertaken informally, and within the life and ministry of my local community in Washington, DC. I think that this is a great model, one that we ought to develop and celebrate. Through it I was exposed to ideas, theologies and spiritualities—which ranged from the orthodox to the outright heretical—not as inert studies, but from engaging with those who lived them. A substantive difficulty with this model of clergy preparation, however, is the fact that it requires a stable community (an elusive goal in many OC/IC congregations and synods), and a level of scholarship already extant within the community, to be able to pass on the necessary body of knowledge and experiences to empower candidates to confidently carry out ordained service. While I have personally enjoyed and benefited from my university experiences, it was something that I wanted to do for myself, rather than something my community required of me. However, throughout my academic life my community has been a great support and resource. In our all-volunteer movement, it is unreasonable to expect that all clergy will have a theology degree. That being said, I think it is also unreasonable for us not to expect a high level of scholarship within the community (not just clergy) that continues to develop and celebrate our OC/IC ethos and heritage, providing theological, liturgical, and historical resources to believers.

I celebrated the thirteenth anniversary of my election and consecration in 2008. When I began this journey, I never imagined the adventure that lay before me, with its moments of exhilarating pride and depressing disappointments. Through my involvement in the ministry of ordained service, I have had opportunities and experiences I do not think would have been possible were it not for my involvement in the OC/IC community. While I might have eventually returned to finish my first degree, I doubt I would have gone to Oxford to study Old Catholic history (indeed, I nearly did not go but for the urging of my parishioners and friends). These are two events that have had a positive influence on how I live my faith and, I think, on how I can best fulfil the role of my office.

There is, of course, another side to this story. Neither the community of St. Mary Magdalene, the first parish I joined at the beginning of this journey nearly twenty years ago, nor my own parish of Sts. Cyril and Methodius, have endured. The fact that these two assemblies no longer exist is disappointing, as both made a substantive contribution to my faith and the shape of my ministry. Both communities, however, have one thing in common: they accurately reflect the curious, sometimes very frustrating story of communities across the OC/IC movement. Why this is so I think is worth a wider discussion, but one thing does stand out, and that is the role of bishops. Back in the second century, St. Ignatius said that where the bishop is, the church is. Our movement is heavily dependent on bishops in a way that does not appear to affect other contemporary sacramental traditions. If, in a community, a bishop moves or dies, the likelihood that that particular ministry will then dissolve is very high. When I moved to London in 1998, my community in Washington collapsed even though I feel it had the skills, resources, and ordained ministers to continue. When Bishop Tom Clary moved to California from Washington, what remained of St. Mary Magdalene parish disappeared. Similarly, the story of the FCCI reflects the stories of synods across the spectrum of our movement—if one bishop dissents or disrupts the frequently tense balance of theologies and ideologies within that community, the whole house collapses.

It might be argued that this inability to maintain a consistent presence and build on the work of others in the same community, is largely due to a lack of leadership skill. I think that there is some truth to this in the movement as a whole, but it is not the whole story. I've been involved in volunteer organisations most of my life, and I have even been involved in founding chapters and branches, as well as founding one organisation, Malchus (which was a monthly zine of news and theology for LGBT Christians), outright. These all had that elusive staying power. For years prior to my leaving Washington, I encouraged people in the community to take leadership roles, knowing that eventually either I would move out of the area or one of them would and could possibly plant a new community. Part of my preparation to move to the UK was to meet with members of my parish in Washington to ensure that they had everything needed to continue the ministry without me. Within a month of my leaving, the community had dissipated. I think there are at least three very challenging hurdles to overcoming this problem; all are related to the fact that many in the movement (unless ordained) do not have a strong sense of sharing a unique OC/IC identity. First of all, many communities actively cultivate an argument "justifying" our "legitimacy" and "existence" based on ideologies of other churches, rather than on our own independent scholarship and thinking. The hope is to attract disaffected members of other sacramental churches. The problem is that they may come, but most will maintain a religious identity grounded in another church community rather than ours. Secondly, many people in our communities do not often "convert" but merely "attend" and "participate." Thus, since they are not invested in the vision and values of the ministry, they are not necessarily concerned about its long-term survival. While it lasts, they are happy to enjoy it; but once it leaves, they will equally be happy to look elsewhere. Finally, there is a widespread problem in Christianity as a whole, and that is the fact that in most congregations, a few highly engaged, committed, active people run everything, and barring that, the priest (or pastor) does. In our OC/IC context this model is simply un-workable; *everyone* has to take an active role in the life of a community if it is to flourish. Throughout my episcopal ministry, I have struggled unsuccessfully with all three of these hurdles. I think that until we manage to find ways to surmount them, we will always have a movement heavily reliant on one (possibly two, if you acknowledge the significance of priests in maintaining some communities) of the four orders, rather than the entire assembly. This is in some ways a disturbing realisation, raising questions about how we embody authentic catholicity.

With the exception of myself, none of the original members of my synod, which began in 1993, are still a part of the community. The story of the highs and lows of my particular synod is also a reflection of the stories of so many synods struggling to get on in our unique circumstances. Some came into my community expecting personal advancement and the acquisition of status. Realising that we don't work that way, they left. Others see our OC/IC communities as a bridge between Christianity and neo-paganism, neo-gnosticism, and other non-Christian spiritualities. They are with us for a time, letting go of the remnants of their Christian faith before moving on. Still others (usually Roman Catholics, Anglicans, and Orthodox) come to us for a time as refugees from their particular "Big-Tent Church." Eventually, they return home or abandon Christianity altogether. In short, while I do think that this situation might be changing, it is often the case that people avoid the psychological and emotional shift from merely participating in a particular parish or ministry to claiming membership in the OC/IC tradition. This fluidity of association can be accommodated in traditions with a larger membership roll, and established institutions. In our context, however, it creates real challenges to community building and even short-term and long-term planning in local ministries. When there are not enough people in the community who actually "own" their membership and who are not merely participants, planning community projects, gatherings, and engagement with other OC/IC communities is frustrating.

A number of friends who are also bishops, having repeatedly struggled with the frustrations of community building and the challenges that come with managing personalities, competing agendas, and non-compatible theologies and having been badly burned in the process, have abandoned entirely the project of community building. They have instead turned to prayer, study, and celebrating liturgy alone, quietly ministering to others when and as they are able. Prayer, study, and quiet Christian witness (through service and presence) ought to be, I think, core elements in every OC/IC believer's spiritual practice. I am, however, a strong advocate of the theology of ordained service as an office grounded in, and exercised among, the local community of believers. Priests in my community, for example, are forbidden to celebrate the Eucharist unless the community is present, and by community I mean living people, not angels! While I disagree with the practice of sole celebration of the Eucharist, I can certainly sympathise with my fellow clergy, who, having given it their all, found that the struggle to overcome some of the hurdles which come with living in our movement has left them tired, even disillusioned.

I cannot imagine myself living my faith in any other tradition; this is my home. While I readily admit that we are sometimes our own worst enemy, the fact is that this is no different from the experience of other traditions. Along with fellow bishops, I have sought to find new and effective ways of exercising this ministry that remain authentically Christian, that celebrate our unique and colourful heritage and that overcome at least some of the challenges presented by our choosing to be OC/IC believers. I have had moments of success and many reversals, but the mission continues.

The Most Rev. Dr.
Carol P. Vaccariello

Old Catholic Order
of Holy Wisdom

# "A Mighty Wind of Blessing and Becoming"

*Life book cracked open*
*Mystery on ev'ry page*
*Eyes blinded with now!*

IT WAS A WINTRY DAY IN 1954. A group of third graders were out on the playground of Saint Margaret Mary's Roman Catholic Church/School in a tight huddle around our visiting missionary priest. Without thought or warning my eyes caught his and I said with certainty and the determination of innocence, "Some day Father, I'm going to be a priest just like you!" He looked at me with his deep grey eyes and said, "Honey, you can't be a priest, but some day you can be a sister." Feeling a deep pain in my chest, I clenched my teeth and walked away saying, "NO! I'm going to be a PRIEST, JUST LIKE YOU!" That was the beginning of a long and circuitous journey, full of adventure, wonder, questions, longing, passion, tears of sorrow and tears of joy, creativity, and transformation.

For all of my life I have continually sought to live the life to which I have felt called.

In the seventh grade I began playing the organ and sang for three Latin Masses each morning before going to school. I became the Sisters' assistant Sacristan, especially taking care of everything during the summers when the nuns were away. Preparing for Mass, being certain the paraments were the correct color for the day or season, changing the "clothes" on the Infant of Prague, marking the ritual books for the Mass of the day, laundering the priests' albs and laying out their vestments each day, filling the chalice and preparing the hosts, and more…. This was a very sacred role in my young years. These tasks were my deep prayer and formed my soul in longing for all that is Holy.

My parents believed in nurturing my gifts and I attended the Cleveland Institute of Music and the Music School Settlement from an early age to learn piano, solfeggio (a method of sight reading new music), and music theory which prepared me to begin Conservatory studies at a college level while completing my last year of High School. This acceleration allowed me to accept a church musician's position at Saint Marion's Roman Catholic Church, an Italian ethnic parish, when I was in High School.

My life was steeped in spirituality and ritual. I loved my church and my God and my Jesus. My heart was on fire with a call to ministry—a call in all of its fullness. The Roman Catholic Church had no room for my call to priesthood. They encouraged me to join the convent. I became a Sister of the Holy Humility of Mary and lived that life—a very good and rich life that taught me the depth of prayer and spiritual practice that I don't believe

I could have learned or experienced anywhere else. I will always be grateful for those years. In my heart of hearts I knew that this wasn't the all of it for me. I needed to keep searching for a way to respond to the still small persistent voice of Spirit.

Five years later, I left Villa Maria and once again began my search to live the call that I felt. I piled on the learning, earning a Bachelor of Arts in Music Education, a Master of the Science of Education to be a Guidance Counselor with a minor in Religious Education, a Masters in Business Administration and the equivalent of a Masters in Divinity followed by a Doctor of Ministry with a speciality in Dream Work as a Spiritual Practice.

I taught religion in Roman Catholic schools, did guidance counseling, tutored music students to create new forms of music and ritual for worship and led small spirituality groups among high school students.

Earning my MBA in participative management opened more doors and opportunities in corporate America as an executive in a leading retail business. I now apply my participative management skills at the University level and the Churches where I am called to pastor.

Earning the Music Degree and studying Liturgical Music at the Conservatory Level helped me to serve a number of churches as Director of Liturgy and Sacred Music. I provided much of the ritual and prayer opportunities for the congregations, just as any parish priest is called to do, yet I was restricted from the call that I felt so clearly. I served three different Roman Catholic Churches in full time positions and too many to mention as supply musician. I was also called to serve the Diocesan Liturgical Music Commission by the Bishop of Cleveland and was sent as a delegate to the Eucharistic Congress in Philadelphia, PA in 1976 where I had the opportunity to hear Mother Theresa speak. I was very Roman Catholic and loved being what I was born to be.

The inner piercing of my heart I experienced in third grade never ceased and I continued to search for how I was to fulfil that call. One day I was contacted to help out at a Christian Church, Disciples of Christ (DOC) in Novelty, Ohio. Their organist was vacationing and they needed a musician to step in. Friends invited me to come and I did. I had never heard of the Disciples of Christ before so this was truly a first time experience for me. The next time that I was called to help out at this same church, they had a new minister who had been filling the pulpit for just a few weeks before I came to provide and lead the music. I strummed my guitar and sang a song titled "Lord, Teach Us To Pray" when something quite extraordinary happened. The church became so still that I needed to open my eyes to see if anyone was still there. When I was finished singing my legs felt weak and I sat down immediately. Then the new minister came to the pulpit and looking directly at me said, "I don't know what it is, Carol, but when you sing the Spirit stirs!" That week he called and invited me to come to his office to talk.

This was the first time in my entire life that a *man* asked me what I was doing about my calling. He affirmed me and offered to be my sponsor to the Ordained Ministry of the Disciples of Christ. I had been so accustomed to being discounted and pushed aside that I had a difficult time taking it all in....and then, it was what I refer to as my own personal Pentecost. On Easter of that year I came forward to join the Disciples of Christ.

My one and true Baptism was as an infant in the Roman Catholic Church. On the feast of Pentecost in 1984, I was baptized by immersion as is the practice of the Disciples of Christ. I chose to do this as a renewal of my Baptismal vows and so that I would know the experience that I would be administering for others. Within the year following that Pentecost 1984, I spent some time getting to know the polity of the Disciples of Christ. That summer, the Reverend Kenneth Hayes, my sponsor, scheduled an appointment for me to meet with the Commission on Ministry. After reviewing my College and Convent studies it was determined that I needed to complete three things in order to have everything in place for Ordination. These included a course in Disciples' polity from a well established minister in the region, a homiletics course, and to become involved in the life of a local church.

In my eagerness, I completed all three by December and presented evidence of that to the Regional Minister at our Church Assembly. He was amazed that all had been done in such a short period of time. Seeing that I had in fact completed all of the requirements he gave me the go ahead to set a meeting with the Commission on Ministry on March 19th to determine my readiness for ordination. We met and ordination was set for Pentecost Sunday 1985.

From one Pentecost to the next it was truly a whirlwind of events and planning to meet all of the requirements and to prepare the Ordination Celebration.

With the attainment of the Masters in Divinity equivalency and my Ordination on May 26 1985, I began to serve as an Interim Minister for the Disciples of Christ. I was well prepared for the resistance that I met in my first church around the issue of a "woman clergyperson." I thought I was past this struggle only to find that although the Christian Church (DOC) had a practice of ordaining women there were still a large number of congregations who had deep problems with accepting women clergy. A deep healing was evident when it was time for me to conclude my interim ministry with them. At the farewell service there were many tear-filled eyes that said it all. We had shared the most important kind of love affair and that experience overcame the walls of gender discrimination. Since that time I have come to find deep acceptance with the Disciples of Christ. I was invited to lead the retreat for the Regional Ministers and the General Minister and President of the denomination. I have led many retreats for clergy groups and clergy spouses and laity.

Between 1989 and 1992, I completed a Doctor of Ministry at the Ecumenical Theological Seminary in Detroit, Michigan. This was a very special time for me and I learned more than one can imagine. My focus was on *Dream Work as a Spiritual Practice* and I was privileged to work with Dr. John E. Biersdorf as my Mentor/Advisor. It was such an opening experience preparing me for the next significant part of my spiritual journey. I was challenged with "God Expansion Theology." My ideas about the Holy were stretched and the "childlike" relationship I had nurtured now began to mature and develop in ways that allowed me to grow outside of the box of traditional ways of experiencing the Holy. This was the beginning of a divine adventure that continues and will never end. It became the springboard for the Spiritual Direction Practice that I deeply enjoy. For me, it is a deep privilege to assist others as they begin to open to new ways of understanding and living in relationship with God. As a continuation of this deep awareness, I teach a Graduate level course in Spiritual Direction and the first offering is a course in Dream Work and Mandala Art as Meditation.

One day I received a call from a tour company asking if I would like to co-lead a group of spiritual seekers to Machu Picchu, Peru with Matthew Fox. Thus began a friendship with Creation Spirituality Theologian, Matthew Fox. His first and most famous book is *Original Blessing*, a book that changed my life and the lives of many. He wrote and taught what my heart and soul already knew but had no way to articulate. This was my introduction to the world of Creation Spirituality, which has become the lens through which I view the world.

Creation Spirituality is the foundation for my spiritual life. All of my teaching and preaching is informed by the Principles and Paths of Creation Spirituality. I've listed the Ten Principles which include the Four Paths that form the basis of this ancient spiritual tradition:

1. The universe is basically a blessing, that is, something we experience as good.
2. We can and do relate to the universe as a whole since we are a microcosm of that macrocosm and that this relationship "intoxicates" us (Aquinas).
3. Everyone is a mystic (i.e., born full of wonder and capable of recovering it at any age; of not taking the awe and wonder of existence for granted).
4. Everyone is a prophet, i.e., a "mystic in action" (Hocking) who is called to "interfere" (Heschel) with what interrupts authentic life.
5. That humans have to dig and work at finding their deep self, their true self, their spirit self; thus the role

of spiritual praxis and meditation and community confrontation which can itself be a yoga. If we do not undergo such praxis we live superficially out of fear or greed or addiction or someone else's expectations of us. That salvation is best understood as "preserving the good." (Aquinas).

6. That the journey that marks that digging can be named as a four-fold journey:

*Via Positiva*: delight, awe, wonder, revelry
*Via Negativa*: darkness, silence, suffering, letting go
*Via Creativa*: birthing, creativity
*Via Transformativa*: compassion, justice,
   healing, celebration

7. Everyone is an artist in some way and art as meditation is a primary form of prayer for releasing our images and empowering the community and each of us. Art finds its fulfillment in ritual, the community's art.

8. We are all sons and daughters of God; therefore, we have divine blood in our veins, the divine breath in our lungs; and the basic work of God is: Compassion.

9. Divinity is as much Mother as Father, as much Child as Parent, as much Godhead (mystery) as God (history) as much beyond all beings as in all beings.

10. That we experience that the Divine is in all things and all things are in the Divine (Panentheism) and that this mystical intuition supplants theism (and its child, atheism) as an appropriate way to name our relation to the Divine and experience the Sacred.

> List from *Confessions: The Making of a
> Post-Denominational Priest* by Matthew Fox

Eventually, Matthew invited me to work with him in Oakland, California at the *University of Creation Spirituality*. The works of Meister Eckhart O.P., (1260–1328), German theologian, mystic and philosopher; and Hildegard of Bingen, German mystic, writer and composer (September 16, 1098-1179) are among those that I found most transformational.

The Reverend Doctor Matthew Fox was called into other ministry and I remained with the university throughout its transition now known as Wisdom University. I continue to teach in areas of Spirituality and am privileged to co-create the Spiritual Direction Program with the Reverend Doctor Lauren Artress of Grace Cathedral and Caroline Myss, lecturer, author, and medical intuitive. I act as a consultant to the University and am available as Major Advisor and Dissertation Mentor for students working toward the Doctor of Ministry. Each year the graduating class and I work together creating a meaningful ritual to put closure on their years of study. (There is a sample of the Graduation Ritual registered on YouTube listed under the name of graduate, Peter Shipton.)

As Director of the Doctor of Ministry Program at the University of Creation Spirituality, I worked with some of the world's greatest spiritual teachers and was so privileged to learn from them.

Lives come together for good. We are called in ways that fulfil our deepest longings even unaware. Besides the invitation to work with the University, Matthew lured me with the promise to work with him as Ritual Maker and Ritual Leader for the *Techno Cosmic Mass*. I have always loved meaningful ritual and did much of it very naturally incorporating Medicine Wheel Teaching, Full Moon Meditations, Drumming Circles, and Labyrinth Walks into my work as a Christian Pastor. Matthew was surprised by the variety of ritual art that I brought to the Church. I was simply following the movement of the Holy Spirit and introduced what seemed right and good to feed the spiritually hungry.

Being a member of the Techno Cosmic Mass Planning Team, we met weekly to prepare for the once a month celebration of the Cosmic Christ! What a joy and what a feat it was to do this huge undertaking of praise and prayer in a deeply ecumenical and interfaith gathering. The Mass is a reinvention of the Roman Catholic Mass, thus the name. The ritual moves through the Four Paths of Creation Spirituality: The Path of Awe and Wonder (Via Positiva), the Path of Emptiness and Sorrow (Via Negativa), the Path of Creative expression and Union with the Divine (Via Creativa), the Path of Transformation and Justice (Via Transformativa).

The Ritual leadership of the TCM developed and it became evident that the Path of Emptiness and Sorrow was the most difficult to lead and to bring the gathering through the spiritual dynamics. I took responsibility for this leadership role and trained people to work with me in making this very critical Path real and accessible for the ritual participants. I have created and continue to create these Cosmic Ritual experiences around the United States and Canada.

Throughout the time that I spent with the University and the Techno Cosmic Mass, I also pastored churches as an Interim Minister specializing in the healing of deeply wounded congregations. The title that was affectionately given to me by the Regional Minister in California was "Pastor-Healer" and it has become a self-fulfilling prophecy. Each of the churches which I have been called to since that time have been deeply wounded, needing some one to love them and care for their woundedness in profound ways so that they might prepare themselves to invite a full time permanent pastor. I have served in a variety of denominations as I hang on to the "tail of the kite" for dear life. The Holy Spirit fills the kite and off we go to adventures and experiences not yet dreamed! My job is simply to hold on!

First Christian Church in El Paso , Texas learned what it meant to hold on to the tail of the kite. When interviewing for the Senior Minister position, I was quite clear that I would not be like any other pastor that they have known and that if they didn't want an unique experience they needed to consider someone else. The Pastoral Search Committee received this as an invitation to adventure. At the first board meeting of forty-eight members, I suggested that we invite the Tibetan Buddhist Monks to our church for a time of sharing their gifts and talents with us and the community. There was absolute silence in the room! No one wanted to believe what they just heard. Then I firmly confronted them with the reminder that calling me to be their pastor was not an action to be taken lightly and that things would be different. They took a deep breath in unison and gave me the go ahead.

That week I contacted the Monks inviting them to come and spend some time with us. The person that I spoke with was more than a little confounded, asking if I was the pastor of a Christian church? Of course I responded in the affirmative. The voice on the other end of the phone wanted to know if I was sure about this because no other Christian Church had ever invited them. Here are a couple of Haikus that capture the event:

*Thirteen of them came*
*Monks cooking in my kitchen*
*Sleeping on the floor*

*Content and happy*
*Christians and Buddhists as one*
*At their parting, tears.*

March 2003, I was attending a Clergy Retreat when a man whom I had never met approached me. He introduced himself as Bishop Fred Jones of the Old Catholic Church. He said that he knew about my life story and wanted to share some information that might help me to heal my relationship with the Catholic Church and in essence to "come home." We sat and I listened to the story of the Old Catholic Church and the Independent Catholic Movement, of which I was not in the slightest aware! He invited me to consider working with him and to be received as an Independent Catholic Priest. I did that in March of 2003. The recognition of my ordination took place at St. Victor's in Vallejo, California. Bishop Kenneth Barbuta and Bishop Jack Isbell joined Bishop Fred Jones in the ordination ceremony.

During the Recognition of Ordination celebration a very curious thing happened. At the beginning of the service I prepared a bowl of smudge to bless the sacred space. Placing sage, sweet grass, lavender, copal and cedar into an abalone shell, I struck a match and lit the mixture, snuffing the flames to allow the smoke to fill and bless the space. When I had completed the blessing with the smudge I placed it on the steps near the pulpit where I knew it would soon stop smoldering. That's when the miracle happened. Any one who smudges knows that the smoke does not continue to rise if the mixture isn't fanned and coaxed. That celebration lasted over an hour and the smudge was still releasing significant prayers of smoke. Many commented on the continued prayers of the smudge bowl! Bishop Jack, who has Native Blood, made special note of this unexpected blessing.

I was asked to consider the position of Bishop. I didn't really want to think about this since the very thought wreaked of patriarchal hierarchy, of which I wanted no part. Bishop Jones asked me to pray about it and let him know. He said that he wanted me to consider this since I had a lot to teach other Bishops about how to be egalitarian and *not* hierarchal. This was a deep plunge for me. I prepared to make a pilgrimage to my "homeland" of Sicily in search of the meaning and the purpose of my life and these continuous requests to take paths that I had not sought out.

While in Sicily, I visited the Basilica of the Black Madonna in the northern coastal town of Tindari. It was here that I had a very powerful experience. I walked into the rear of the huge Basilica. It was so out of place on the Sicilian countryside. I didn't even want to be there because of all of the vendors and commercialism. Remember, I had come on this pilgrimage to learn more about my roots and what they had to do with the calling and purpose of my life as I was feeling pushed and pulled. It was near the end of our journey and I was unaware of anything significant in the way of new knowledge or guidance in making any intelligent decisions around the invitation to be consecrated Bishop. I had even been visiting jewellery stores along the route to see if perchance the amethyst bishop's ring would present itself in this, the land of my ancestors.

So there I was in the back of the Basilica while a Mass was going on in the front. The statue of the Black Madonna was held up over the main altar by four exquisite ebony Angels. However, it was impossible to see the Black Madonna from where I was standing because of the glare and reflection of the evening light on the plexiglass protection that surrounded her. Without any warning, I felt my feet stuck to the floor as if nailed there. I couldn't move and I heard this voice in my heart of hearts. It was a voice that I had never heard before and it was very clear, pronounced, direct, and waited for no reply. "Hey Girl, I need for you to go do this thing for me. Now, go on and do it!"

This was a voice that didn't ask for a response. There was no place for that. This was the voice of the Black Madonna, the Divine manifest in the Sacred Feminine. I was so shaken that I had to catch my breath. I waited till the Mass was over and then walked to the front to see the statue. Soon I went out of the Basilica to the nearest vendor selling images of the statue and I purchased one to remember her and her powerful and direct message. I had received what I had come to Sicily for. Not in a way that I expected, but definitely in a way that I understood.

Our last day in Sicily before taking the Ferry Boat from Palermo to Naples to board the plane home, we visited Taormina, an exclusive resort village set gently in the hillside. This was my last opportunity to find an amethyst bishop's ring in my ancestral homeland of Sicily. I walked into the last jewellery store that was there. This was a store which I had avoided because I knew the prices would be out of sight in this very exclusive shop. Once inside the two women who spoke only Italian and myself who speaks only English attempted communication. First, I had to explain that in America I was a Catholic priest, something that is truly a foreign concept to them. Once they got that then I went for the next unbelievable truth— that I was about to be consecrated a Bishop and I needed a ring—not just any ring—but an amethyst ring that wasn't covered with gingerbread filigree. One of them got it! She went to a special locked case removing what is now my Bishop's Ring, the symbol of the office and the call to heal. It was a magnificent ring; one that seemed too pretentious for me. The clerk insisted that this was to be my ring and showed me how it would fit and be very special. She was right, of course! Then I thought – there is probably no way that I can afford this gorgeous stone. But as you already know, when the Spirit is involved everything is possible and the ring's price tag was less than some of the rings that I had considered back home. I knew that this ring was the seal on the sacred commissioning to "go do this thing!"

On July 23, 2004, I was consecrated Bishop Sophia by the Old Catholic Church.

After the Consecration I wondered what was so important, what was I to do with this newly created designation, what was the "thing" that I was to "go and do?"

A dear friend, Father John Mabry, asked me to meet with him to discuss something that was close to his heart. We had a long and fruitful conversation about the beginnings of a Religious Order that would be unique in the fact that all members regardless of position had equal vote in all matters. This meant that Bishop/Abbot/Abbess /Priest/Deacon/Lay members all have equal vote in matters of the Order. We started this one-of-a-kind group which continues to thrive today.

It became necessary for me to relocate. Since I was no longer in the Bay Area and the Order of Holy Wisdom needed spiritual leadership, Father John Mabry was consecrated Bishop, becoming Abbot of the Order. I continue to be a part of their work and growth, as I am able.

Much of my delight in my calling of spiritual leader is that of spiritual director or coach. I believe that my many gifts in this area must continue to be offered to those seeking spiritual growth and communion with God. I have witnessed the love of God in so many ways that there is nothing else that I would rather do than be a witness to that great love.

For many important reasons, I have relocated to Ohio to be closer to family and to pay attention to the call of Spirit. I marvel at all that is presenting itself to me in this place that is my birth place. The house that I purchased is much too large for me, because I vision it to be the beginnings of a spiritual community and a place for spiritually hungry souls to come for retreat and rest. I have the privilege of working with many who are seeking greater communion with God. I provide Spiritual Direction one on one, face to face, through telephone communication and email. God is full of surprises and I am holding on securely to the tail of the kite as the Spirit blows the mighty wind of blessing and becoming.

The Rt. Rev. Wynn Wagner

North American
Old Catholic Church

# "All This and Heaven Too"

JESUS WAS A RADICAL. If my marching orders are to live my life like Jesus, I'm supposed to be what? A right-wing bigot? A milk-toast liberal?

The religions I grew up with weren't radical. Mother was a Southern Baptist, and dad's religion-of-the-month gave me inside looks at the Roman Rite and Buddhism.

I was a Southern Baptist for about a week in the 1950s. The readings I heard were fine, even with the Thee's and Thou's. I remember the people were stuffy and eager to point out faults, but I could have gotten past that. But one Sunday morning came a lecture about sex and affection, and it was a show-stopper. Even as a kid I knew that I was gay, and Southern Baptists don't like gay kids. In fact, I never "came out of the closet" because I was never in one. Being gay was just who I was, and if the Southern Baptists had issues with that then I had issues with them.

God simply doesn't make mistakes on such a scale.

Years later, I learned that the Southern Baptists pulled away from the general Baptist group over slavery. The Southern branch thought slavery was just dandy and objected when the national group suggested it is un-Christian. A whole church formed to support slavery. And knowing their beginnings, holier-than-y'all pronouncements from Southern Baptist preachers ring hollow.

Slavery and homophobia is radical, but it is the wrong kind of radical—at least to me. To their credit, I saw an apology on the Southern Baptist website. As a denomination, they said, "Oops, our bad." It took over a hundred years, but they did apologize. I haven't ever seen an apology to all the gay teenagers they've demeaned.

Roman Catholics (RC) were better by degree. In their defense, any group that can claim William Shakespeare, Gracie Allen, Rene Descartes, W. A. Mozart, and the Liber Usualis (Gregorian chant) is a group that demands my respect. The RCs have had such rebel rousers as the Berrigan brothers and Richard Rohr in the rank of clergy, and they know how to stand up against injustice.

The Romans are also anti-gay, but they didn't say so when I was a kid. In fact the reason I bolted and ran from them is due to sex. Their priests and brothers kept wanting in my pants. That fact didn't bother me, but they had promised to be celibate. If you say you won't have sex, then you need to refrain from making passes at the youngsters. By the time three RC clergy had "had their way" with me, I stopped hanging around there.

The Roman rite is the largest Christian sect in the world. They have a billion adherents. I don't want to bash this group for two reasons: first, I'm not sure I could do a better job of keeping a billion fiercely independent people flying in close formation; and two, as a general rule, it is probably safest not to piss off that many people. Imagine a million really pissed-off nuns running after you, waving rulers menacingly.

A billion people gunning for you...it boggles the mind. It has happened before. Remember Galileo Galilei? He made some astronomical observations that annoyed the Romans, and guess who blinked? It wasn't The Church, for heaven's sake.

The Romans finally recognized that science has moved on. It took Rome 400 years to apologize to Galileo. What's more, with all their hateful speech, the Southern Baptists are the first to hit the road to help after a natural disaster.

I was a Buddhist because dad was a Buddhist for a while. I was never a very good Buddhist, and that was my fault not theirs. I was far more interested in motorcycles and teenage puppy love. My hometown had an underage "bar" where I could dance with my boyfriend while downing non-alcoholic drinks. I'm still into motorcycles and downing non-alcoholic drinks, and I've been living with the same guy for years.

Buddhism got me out of serving in Vietnam. From then to now, I looked at a few other Reality Maps, the most notable being the religion of the Pharaohs. One day, I was minding my own business, poking around the internet, looking for something involving the library in Alexandria. Up pops "St. Clement of Alexandria," who was one of the first deep thinkers of the Christian sect. He was the supposed author of an inconvenient little letter that suggests there is a Secret Gospel of Mark and that it might say "naked man with naked man." An ancient same-gender love? An old initiation rite? Scholars have opinions on who said what and when, but nobody has any real evidence. But it got me poking around, and up pops St. Clement of Alexandria Liberal Catholic Church (SCALCC) in nearby Frisco, Texas. The Liberal Catholics came from the Old Catholic Church in Holland. The Liberals, mainly Brits and Aussies at first, included Charles W. Leadbeater and Annie Besant. I knew their work: way out there where the buses don't run. With Leadbeater, you have to drop breadcrumbs or you get lost, but I knew the territory.

I drove up to their parish to kick the tires. SCALCC met in a Holiday Inn. They were friendly and seemingly not judgmental, and their liturgy was straight out of the 1600s. Toward the end of Mass, the priest said "Ite, missa est," and I felt an instant, unmistakable, and stark change in the energy in the room. I had no idea what happened, and I didn't think they did. I went back the next week to see what was going on. What I noticed there was a slow and steady buildup of buzzy energy. Just before the consecration of the bread and wine, the buzzy energy went pop, forming a kind of bubble. Inside the bubble, the energy was intense. Then at the "Ite, missa est" the whole energy bubble exploded outward, replaced by an intense quiet. I have no clue how "quiet" can be "intense," but that's what I felt. These people obviously needed adult supervision. Could they know what they were playing with?

After a few weeks of Sunday Masses in the suburban motel, someone mentioned the LCC seminary. It was a distance-learning thing that I could take or leave as I wanted. In other words, there was no upfront commitment. I ran through a quick personal inventory:

- conscientious objector
  (in Texas, for crying out loud) check
- openly gay (in the Bible belt) check
- use tarot for meditation
  (and too stupid to hide that fact) check

I decided that I didn't have enough people gunning for me, so:

- Liberal Catholic
  (when people are abandoning Christianity in droves)

What else could I do?

I became a priest of the Liberal Catholic Church International. Our parish in Dallas—www.MychalJudge .com—is named after the New York Fire Department chaplain killed on 9/11. Father Mychal was a tireless worker for addicts and drunks. He was always available to help people with HIV and AIDS, and he was about as openly gay as a Franciscan priest can be. To the best of my knowledge, he was always celibate, but he identified him-self as gay.

After a few years, the parish asked me to consider becoming independent of the larger denomination. Because priests always work under a bishop and because the parish wanted to be its own deal, I needed to be a bishop.

Happily I knew three Indy bishops who cast their lots with my flock's sedition. They made me a bishop, and I promised everyone that I wouldn't act like a bishop.

And so, here I sit: an informal cut-off-wearing bishop, gay but with a pointy hat, and following a rite with intri-cate rubrics. It makes no sense, which is why it works!

Jesus was a radical. I don't see how you can follow Jesus but cause harm to others, so I am a steadfast pacifist. Yet our parish has hawkish members, and there's room for both. Maybe you can support war, but I don't see it. They say the same thing about pacifism.

Jesus was a radical. I don't see how you can follow Jesus but keep His Sacraments available only to those who are close to perfect. If you are in a state of sin, you can't do anything except confess? If your parents are divorced, you can't be baptized or confirmed? Who put these latter-day Sadducees in charge?

I won't ask about a person's worthiness before performing Last Rites. We have open communion. I have married male/female and male/male couples, and I didn't make harsh judgement against the male/female couple. They were born with the heterosexual gene. Pitiful, of course, but they can't help it!

Know that story about friends lowering their friend into a house where Jesus was teaching? The fellow could not walk, but his friends knew that Jesus could fix it. What the gospel didn't say was that the guy was a Big Shot in the community, and I think it would have said so if he were. The gospel didn't mention anything about the guy's past. He might have been a serial killer. It omits any news of his future, so he probably remained just a regular guy. He wasn't required to make promises or pass tests. No, our Lord merely tells him to get up and go home. Acting like there was nothing wrong with the man in the first place, Jesus even tells him to drag his bed home with him. When Luke tells the story (Lk 5:17-26), it offers up one of the best understatements in the Bible. Someone in the crowd said, "We have seen strange things today!"

How did we get from the gospel's simple message to the modern rules and canons?

The lesson of the gospel—as I see it—is a message of orthopraxis (correct action), not orthodoxy (correct ideas). Who did our Master fuss at in the gospel? The scribes and dot-the-I/cross-the-T types. To everyone else, he offered love. It isn't what you think, it is what you do, feeding the poor, clothing the naked, anointing the sick, and visiting the incarcerated.

Jesus was a radical. And if you look at what we are supposed to be doing, it is hanging out and helping all the wrong kinds of people. We are to offer ourselves to the sick and the unclean and the criminal element.

Jesus said we're supposed to love God, love ourselves, and love our enemies. He said that all the other rules follow from this principle.

Jesus was a radical, and I do my best to be one, too. My main job lately is doing Unction and Viaticum. The hospital is owned and operated by the Southern Baptists, and I get called when the regular Roman priest is unavailable. The Romans and the Baptists again. Oy: don't try to tell me that God doesn't have a sense of humor.

I'm a conscientious objector / openly gay / tarot-meditating indy catholic bishop using vestments and liturgies that are hundreds of years old.

When I explain all that to the typical Bub, I get an almost perfect deer-in-the-headlights expression coming back. When I see the "huh?"—face, I know that I've taken a layer of phlegm off his view of the world. When I see that face from the red-neck, the orthopraxis is complete. All this and heaven too.